IMAGES OF ENGLAND

THE WREKIN HILL

IMAGES OF ENGLAND

THE WREKIN HILL

ALLAN FROST

For my wife Dorothy, and 'To all friends round The Wrekin'

Frontispiece: Map of The Wrekin and surrounding hills, Ordnance Survey, 1949, showing their proximity to Wellington and the River Severn, whose course was redirected away from its previous flow northwards into the River Dee as a result of an enormous Ice Age lake overflowing and cutting the gorge at Ironbridge. The river now flows southwards into the Bristol Channel.

First published in 2007 by Tempus Publishing

Reprinted in 2008 by
The History Press
The Mill, Brimscombe Port,
Stroud, Gloucestershire, GL5 2QG
www.thehistorypress.co.uk

Reprinted 2010, 2011, 2012

© Allan Frost 2008

The right of Allan Frost to be identified as the Author of this work has been asserted in accordance with the Copyrights, Designs and Patents Act 1988.

All rights reserved. No part of this book may be reprinted or reproduced or utilised in any form or by any electronic, mechanical or other means, now known or hereafter invented, including photocopying and recording, or in any information storage or retrieval system, without the permission in writing from the Publishers.

British Library Cataloguing in Publication Data.
A catalogue record for this book is available from the British Library.

ISBN 978 0 7524 4256 3

Typesetting and origination by Tempus Publishing.
Printed and bound in Great Britain.

Contents

	Acknowledgements	6
	Introduction	7
one	Myth and Legend	9
two	Facts, not Fantasy	19
three	Early Settlers	25
four	Hill Economies	31
five	Beacons and the BBC	41
six	The Halfway House	51
seven	The Forest Glen	65
eight	People's Playground and Paraphernalia	79

Acknowledgements

Many people, organisations and various sources have contributed information and illustrations for this book, including the Author's collection, Barbers, T. Bolger, I. Dormor, G. Evans, B. and C. Felton, A. Fisher, D. Frost, D.L. Frost, P. Garbett, Green Wood Trust, A. Gregory, A. Grundy, A. Heighway, Ironbridge Gorge Museum, F. Jones, P. Lambert, K. Lewis, P. Luter, M. McCrea, W. Newbold, B. O'Loughlin, C. Overton, M. Petty, C. Powell, G. Riley, R. Tranter, T. Tyrer, *Salopian Shreds & Patches*, Shrewsbury Records and Research Library, Shropshire Hills Discovery Centre, *Shropshire Star*, *Telford Journal*, Shropshire Wildlife Trust, *Wellington Journal & Shrewsbury News*, Wellington Library, *Wellington News*, *Wellington Standard* and R. & D. Vickers.

I am most grateful to them all, as well as for the continued forbearance of my wife Dorothy, and apologise sincerely to anyone who has been inadvertently omitted. Every effort has been made to correctly identify the facts, dates, events and people portrayed in the illustrations.

Hog's back view of The Wrekin from the south-west in the 1930s with The Little Hill projecting just above the trees in the centre. The village of Eaton Constantine across the centre witnessed several crashes during the Second World War when aircraft clipped the top of the hill or flew into overhead wires.

Introduction

The Wrekin Hill is not just any hill. It somehow represents the spirit of Shropshire and a visit to its ancient slopes takes on the feeling of a spiritual pilgrimage. Although not the highest hill in the county it is one of the most impressive, rising as it does from the levels of the north Shropshire Plain to signal the eastern border of the South Shropshire Hills.

The Wrekin forms the north-eastern extremity of the Shropshire Hills Area of Outstanding Natural Beauty (AONB): 802sq kms of England's finest countryside. The AONB, which was designated in 1958, also includes Wenlock Edge, the Stretton Hills, the Long Mynd, the Stiperstones, Clun Forest and the Clee Hills.

The Wrekin is not quite a mountain, which strictly must rise at least 1,000ft above the surrounding countryside before qualifying for that title, but it is no less impressive despite this minor shortcoming. If any hill in Shropshire is to be climbed, it has to be this one; the panoramic views from its summit are superb, breathtaking and impressive, opening a unique window on the South Shropshire Hills, the Roman ruins at Wroxeter, the Severn Gorge, the northern plain and the West Midlands.

There are countless reasons why The Wrekin and its neighbouring hills are regarded with undying affection by Salopians (and others) the world over. Throughout the millennia it has been a source of refuge, a means of livelihood, an important social amenity – and the scene of personal injury and, on occasion, death.

Oddly enough, it is always referred to as *The* Wrekin, as if to emphasise its unique position in the minds of generations, not just as *Wrekin* in the way we refer to Snowdon, Ben Nevis or Scafell Pike. What it lacks in stature is more than compensated for by the important place it occupies in people's hearts.

How the hill came to hold such a power for so long over the people living in its shadow is impossible to say. Perhaps it's because it doesn't seem to threaten the inhabitants and appears to offer them some form of supernatural protection. Certainly, when viewed from the north, it takes on the appearance of a long, sleeping dragon, whose head is represented by The Little Hill at the south-western slope. Note that the names of The Little Hill and, at the opposite end of The Wrekin, The Ercall are both preceded by the definite article when referred to by locals, unlike other hills in the area (such as Maddock's and Lawrence), although some Ordnance Survey maps ignore this fact.

Viewed from the south-west, The Wrekin takes on a completely different appearance, usually described as a hog's back which, from a visual point of view, is more impressive but misleads the visitor into thinking the whole hill covers a relatively small area. They are somewhat surprised to find the ascent from the Forest Glen is a little further and slightly more strenuous than expected.

The Wrekin Hill holds many attractions for walkers and nature lovers; the well-trodden trackways are not too arduous, although the upper stretches from the Halfway House to the summit require a little more effort – effort that will be well rewarded.

The hill is full of surprises and natural beauty; its history, like that of its neighbouring hills, is fascinating. I hope this book goes some way to explain why the area has meant and continues to mean so much to so many over such a long period.

Allan Frost
Priorslee, Shropshire

Western end of The Wrekin as seen from the north with The Little Hill attached on the right, 2005. It is this side of the hill that, with a little imagination, resembles a sleeping dragon waiting for a call to help the inhabitants of Wellington.

Aerial view of the north side of The Wrekin Hill with The Little Hill in the foreground and The Ercall in the far distance, 1930s. Note the partial absence of trees on the flank at that time.

one
Myth and Legend

Everyone knows The Wrekin Hill itself and a few of its features were made by giants. Unfortunately, which giants they were and quite how they came to build the hill in the first place is open to debate. Similarly, we do not know exactly when the hill was created but we do know it was some time before Bronze Age settlers entered the area approximately 3,000 years ago because they built a fort around the summit.

There are three basic versions of how giants built both The Wrekin Hill and The Ercall. Each story was well established in folklore when they were 'formalised' in the 1870s. The first goes like this:

> Long, long ago, in the days when there were giants in the land, two of them were turned out by the rest and forced to go and live by themselves, so they set to work to build themselves a hill to live in. In a very short time they had dug out the earth from the bed of the Severn, which runs in the trench they made to the present time, and with it they piled up The Wrekin, intending to make it their home.
>
> Those bare patches on the turf, between the Bladderstone and the top of the hill, are the marks of their feet, where from that day to this the grass has never grown. But they had not been there long before they quarrelled, and one of them struck at the other with his spade, but failed to hit him, and the spade descending to the ground cleft the solid rock and made the 'Needle's Eye'.
>
> Then they began to fight, and the giant with the spade (for they seem to have had only one between them: perhaps that was what they quarrelled about!) was getting the best of it at first, but a raven flew up and pecked at his eyes, and the pain made him shed such a mighty tear that it hollowed out the little basin in the rock which we call the Raven's Bowl, or sometimes the Cuckoo's Cup, which has never been dry since, but is always full of water even in the hottest summers.
>
> And now you may suppose that it was very easy for the other giant to master the one who had the spade, and when he had done so, he determined to put him where he could never trouble anyone again. So he very quickly built up The Ercall Hill beside the Wrekin, and imprisoned his fallen foe within it. There the poor blind giant remains until this day, and in the dead of night you may sometimes hear him groaning.

The Raven's Bowl behind the author's children Caroline (left) and Tim, 1977. Raven's Bowl is probably a much older name than its alternative, Cuckoo's Cup. Ravens are known to have inhabited the summit until the latter half of the nineteenth century.

Like many myths, there is at least one grain of truth in this tale: the Raven's Bowl, or Cuckoo's Cup as it is also called, very rarely dries up although the water inside does freeze in extremely cold temperatures.

A similar legend actually gives each giant a name. In this story, The Wrekin (presumably built by the giants in the first story) already existed when these events took place:

THE BATTLE OF THE GIANTS

There were two giants that did battle together, for the jealousy that was between them that each had of the other's strength; and the place where they did battle was upon the hill that is called Wrekin. And the greatness of the body of the one giant was such that were he bound in a chain of iron, and the links of the chain an inch in thickness, he burst the chain when he broadened his chest to breathe. And his limbs were so smooth, that there might nothing hold thereto without at first wounding his side, except only his girdle of gold, that had been forged for him by Griffin the smith: and beneath his girdle was the skin of a lion: and for these things he was called Leugh.

And the other giant was covered all in hair as it had been the bristles of a wild boar: and for his great fierceness he was called Tore. Wherefore, as soon as they were come together upon the hill, they grappled each with other, and strove to overcome his enemy by the mightiness of his strength; now one bearing back his foe with the suppleness of his body, and now the other bearing him up on his shoulder by his great strength. From where they fought there smoke rose, and flames burst from their nostrils. Men stood in fear, and said a fire devoured the forests of the hill. Trees they trampled underfoot, and huge stones rolled down the mountainside.

The Raven's Bowl outcrop, as seen looking south-east from the summit, 1920s.

Sobs burst from forth their mouths, and the land was rent, and shook and trembled as they swayed. Then slowly the greater of the two, that was Leugh, bore the other back, inch by inch, and their chests as they heaved together were like the waves that burst upon each other, and run upon the beach, and are drawn in sharply beneath the next that rolls above them.

Then he shot forth his arm and caught the other by the throat, and in the sudden pain thereof, a tear was flung from his eye, and where it fell it bored through the rock, and made a cleft. And the cleft it made is called the Needle's Eye. Then he took him, and clasped his arms to his side, and tore his chest with his teeth as he lay above him. And the giant that lay undermost writhed and strove to be free, but the more he strove the more he felt himself powerless and weak; and he cast his head back, and gave a great cry that men heard far and near and were amazed. But the giant tore his chest and plied mercilessly his eager teeth; and the blood flowed down, and formed a great basin in the hill, and thither flocked a mighty troop of ravens and feasted in the blood of the giant. And it is called the Raven's Bowl to this day.

So Leugh slew Tore, and this is called the Battle of the Giants.

Another version, better known and generally regarded as being more 'accurate' and acceptable, is as follows:

Once upon a time there was a wicked old giant in Wales, who, for some reason or other, had a very great spite against the Mayor of Shrewsbury and all his people, and he made up his mind to dam up the Severn, and by that means cause such a flood that the town would be drowned. So off he set, carrying a spadeful of earth, and tramped along mile after mile, trying to find the way

The Needle's Eye around 1905, as seen from the east, the usual way to enter the cleft. By this time, it had become quite fashionable to take a stroll up The Wrekin, even for well dressed ladies. There were considerably more tall trees growing on the southern slopes of the hill than there are today.

to Shrewsbury. And how he missed it I cannot tell, but he must have gone wrong somewhere, for at last he got close to Wellington, and by that time he was puffing and blowing under his heavy load, and wishing he was at the end of his journey.

By-and-bye there came a cobbler along the road with a sack of old boots and shoes on his back, for he lived at Wellington, and went once a fortnight to Shrewsbury to collect his customers' old boots and shoes, and take them home with him to mend. And the giant called out to him.

'I say,' he said, 'how far is it to Shrewsbury?'

'Shrewsbury!' said the cobbler; 'what do you want at Shrewsbury?'

'Why,' said the giant, 'to fill up the Severn with this lump of earth I've got here. I've an old grudge against the Mayor and the folks at Shrewsbury, and now I mean to drown them out and get rid of them all at once.'

'My word!' thought the cobbler, 'this'll never do! I can't afford to lose my customers!' and he spoke up again. 'Eh!' he said, 'you'll never get to Shrewsbury, not today, nor tomorrow. Why, look at me! I'm just come from Shrewsbury, and I've had time to wear out all these old boots and shoes on the road since I started.' And he showed him his sack.

'Oh!' said the giant, with a great groan, 'then it's no use! I'm fairly tired out already, and I can't carry this load of mine any farther. I shall just drop it here and go back home.'

So he dropped the earth on the ground just where he stood, and scraped his boots on the spade, and off he went home again to Wales, and nobody ever heard anything of him in Shropshire after. But where he put down his load, there stands The Wrekin to this day, and even the earth he scraped off his boots was such a pile that it made the little Ercall by the Wrekin's side.

The western side of the Needle's Eye, 2000. Caroline (left) and Tim have just passed through the cleft and entered the deep gulley which is now blocked by a large pyramid-shaped rock. It fell from the outcrop during an earthquake in May 1990. There are several myths and superstitious beliefs associated with the Needle's Eye.

As if to add credibility to the last version, this anonymous poem first appeared in the September 1875 issue of *Salopian Shreds & Patches*. It firmly places the story in medieval times and is reproduced here:

YE LEGEND OF YE WREKIN

In olden times, when Bards still flourished,
ere Nurse Chivalry had Arthur nourished,
lived in Wales amid the mountain passes,
A Giant, who, among the upper classes
That is, his giant brethren – was thought
Quite a great man; and so he ought;
For in his weight and breadth of figure,
His strength and size, he was a great deal bigger
Than any other giant round about;
And if his size was great, no doubt
His appetite was greater; for he'd eat
Food for an army when he had a treat.
So capacious his maw,
And his powers of jaw,
That he'd eat half a score
Of sheep, or perhaps more,
Though he'd had just before, by way of tit bit,
Just a dozen of turkeys or so on a spit;
While to wash it all down, when he meant to make merry,
He'd empty at least half a hosghead of sherry;
For no teetotaller he, but inclined to be jolly;
He thought drinking water a very great folly;
And, had anyone tried, he'd have thought them insane
To bring in a liquor law over the main,
But though fond of his wine,
He would not decline
A bumper of metheglin,
That liquor divine,
Or even of ale, if the brewing was fine;
Although, down in Wales
They don't talk of their ales,
But spell it, as though 'twere on purpose to trouble you
With a C and a WR, and a W.
A word to pronounce which you'd have some ado,
But the nearest approach to the sound is cooroo;
For to learn the Welsh language if you should choose
You'll W have to pronounce like two Us.

Now, from what I have said as to how he could eat,
You may guess that the neighbourhood thought it no treat
To find such a gourmand as he with his meat;

For he'd ne'er thought of paying for what they provided,
And at all their complainings he only derided;
Until, the supplies running short, he decided
To send further off to obtain his provision,
And thus of his favours made equal division.
So he sent off a message to Shrewsbury's Mayor,
Commanding that he, every week, should prepare
For the Giant's consumption, a pretty good share
Of sheep, pigs and oxen, and other things rare;
And, without fail, to send them to any place where
The said Giant appointed; and if he should dare
Not to send them in time he, the Giant, would swear
That in less than a jiffy he'd surely be there,
And so quash up their city, that all should declare
They never had seen such a sight anywhere.

I don't know, reader, if you've ever been
To Shrewsbury, that quaint and ancient city;
But if it be a place you've never seen,
It's worth a visit for 'tis really pretty;
And round its walls a river runs I ween,
Full often-times the theme of poet's ditty.
If you should go there, I am sure 'twill please ye,
And, in these railway days, the visit's easy.
But, whether you've been then or no, you may guess
Such a message as this put the Mayor in a mess.
So he summon'd the Council without more ado,
And begged that each member would give him his view
As to what, in this difficult case, they should do.
Now the Council, of course, when they met couldn't see
Any single point upon which they'd agree;
So they haggled and boggled, and moved and amended,
Till you'd think the discussion would never be ended;
When a member got up and said if they'd permit, he
Would move that the case be referred to committee;
And, gaining his motion, he begged to propose
Some half dozen gentlemen, who, if they chose,
Would speedily bring the affair to a close,
This, of course, was opposed, and another list started,
And into two parties the council was parted.
The chairman declared that the first list selected
Was by the majority duly elected;
When up jumped a member, and said he objected
On very good grounds to the list as a whole,
On the part of his party, demanding a poll.
This, of course, took up time; and the Giant, meanwhile
Not receiving his grub, was beginning to rile.
He got up one day, in a deuce of a rage.

He blew up his valet, and knocked down his page;
Then rushing downstairs, when his toilet was made,.
And, arming himself with a very large spade,
Dug up a great hill,
Swore he'd give than a pill,
And smother their city for treating him ill.

Now a cobbler, near Shrewsbury, who lived in a stall,
Which served him for kitchen, and parlour, and hall,
(Here some sharp critic may,
With an acid face, say
That last line's not original, though, by the way,
Well, don't be in a fright;
Mr Critic, you're right:
It isn't original; but, without a doubt,
It suits well my verse, so I shan't cross it out).
Now this cobbler was famous the country around
As the very best hand that was anywhere found
At the curing of soles that were getting unsound;
And every fortnight or so he went round
And collected the shoes
That the folks couldn't use
And he got a good heap,
For his charges were very cheap,
Now this Cobbler one morning his way home was wending,
With a pretty good bagful of shoes wanting mending,
When he heard a great sound,
Which shook even the ground;
And, on looking around,
He saw a great mound,
Or rather a mountain, which toward him came.
He at first thought his senses were having a game;
With his eyesight, as Shakespeare once express'd it,
Although, perhaps, in different language he dress'd it.
But, as long as he gaz'd
He was somewhat amazed
To find by a giant the mountain was carried.
So, thinking it wise if he no longer tarried,
He took to his heels, and before one could say
'Jack Robinson', swiftly he bolted away.
When the Giant saw Crispin, he swung out 'halloa!
Down there below,
My fine fellow, don't go;
How far is it to Shrewsbury? I want to know.'
Poor Crispin, on hearing this sound, at once stopped,
Though he thought that with fright he'd have dropped,
And said, 'Sir, I hope you won't take it ill,
If I ask what you are going to do with that hill?'

Said the Giant, 'I've sent down to Shrewsbury there,
To order that precious old donkey, the Mayor,
To provide me with plenty of grub for my dinner.
He's neglected, and surely as I am a sinner.'
(He went on in a voice which made Crispin shiver)
'I've been d-----g their town, so I'll now dam the river,
And then, by its waters the city surrounded,
The whole of the people will surely be drownded.'

Now the Cobbler, who, though in a bit of a flurry,
Couldn't bear such a sin against poor Lindley Murray,
Said, 'They'll surely be killed when the waters surround;
But you shouldn't say drownded – you should have said drowned.'
'Pooh!' the giant replied; 'your objection's unfounded;
They'll be dead when they're drowned,
so of course they'll be drownded.
However, no matter,
Don't make such a clatter,
I'm tired to death, and cannot stop for your chatter.
So tell me at once, without circumlocution,
Or any more hints as to my elocution.
How far may it be
To this said Shrewsbury?'
Says the Cobbler, says he,
'I don't know – let me see –
I can't tell you exactly how far – but I know
That, though with such legs you won't walk very slow,
You won't get there today; or perhaps even tomorrow;
For, in walking from thence, I've found to my sorrow
I've worn out these shoes on my back which I carry,
And which load I was wishing just now on Old Harry.'
The Giant on hearing this, uttered a groan
Would have melted a heart that was not made of stone,
And said, 'Well I'm blowed!
If I'd certainly knowed
'Twas so far, I would never have carried this load.'
Said the cobbler – a second time getting corrective –
'Your grammar, again, sir, I tell you's defective:
You should have said blown,
And if I had known;
For to say blowed and knowed is uncommonly low.'
'Hold your row!' said the Giant, 'or this much I know:
I shall do you some damage; my temper I'm losing,
And the sweat from each pore of my body is oozing;
However, this thing I'll soon get off my hands.'
So he dropped it, and there to this moment it stands.
And if e'er for amusement you're Shrewsbury seeking
You'll find it not far from Shropshire's own Wrekin.

Above left: Postcard from the 1940s, providing a valuable hint that venturing through the Needle's Eye is not for the more portly visitor, especially if he's had a drink or two beforehand to pluck up the courage.

Above right: The Ercall Hill (which also has the remains of a medieval enclosure on its summit) as seen from The Wrekin, looking north-east, *c.* 1900. Several quarries have eaten away at the hill over an extremely long period; that of Lawrence Hill can be seen in the centre foreground. On the left is the partially dried up reservoir, created during the latter years of the nineteenth century to satisfy the fresh water requirements of Wellington, which was experiencing considerable improvements to civic amenities and public health at the time.

View of the northern flank of The Ercall across the full reservoir, *c.* 1905. Ercall Lane, the main route from Wellington to the foot of The Wrekin, runs along the hedgerow across the centre of the picture. The road at the foot of the photograph is the start of Wrekin Course.

two

Facts, not Fantasy

Even with these accepted accounts of the hill's formation, their veracity was called into question by doubting Victorians, who developed a habit of challenging traditional explanations and, after much research, reached scientifically based conclusions which, in their eyes at least, proved that giants had no hand in the matter. It was their search for the truth that led to more unimaginative, less romantic, theories on this famous hill's origins. Considerably more work has been done by post-Victorian geologists using advanced techniques and taking into account the vast amount of knowledge gained from observations made in other parts of the world.

They concentrated their examinations on the variety of rocks and overlying deposits which exist in the area. They came to the conclusion that The Wrekin itself was of volcanic origin but not, in fact, a volcano. A volcano erupts through the ground, spewing out molten lava and ash, as happened in the Church Stretton area to the south-west. The Wrekin appears to have been (in geological terms) a batholith, an enormous accumulation of magma (molten lava) which cooled down before it actually reached the surface. Erosion eventually stripped away the ground above, thus exposing the batholith beneath.

However, whereas The Wrekin itself was not a volcano, there is evidence that lava did reach the surface in places and flowed to form sheets of rock when it cooled down. This was an extremely turbulent period in the earth's history but it would not end there.

The land masses of the earth are in continual motion. Continents float on an unseen sea of magma which causes them to separate and crash against each other. Consequently, an area of land previously bobbing around below the equator could find itself travelling northward to colder climes in a matter of minutes, in geological terms.

During that period of movement, land experiences a range of activity. It might suffer erosion from the sea, it could become submerged, it could run against another land mass and find itself converted into a mountain which may then be eroded by rain, ice or river action. A record of these phenomenal changes is stored, not only within the rocks themselves but also in the way they appear at present and the types of rock formed at each stage in their endless journey. Eventually, they will change again; it is a constant process.

An excellent example of just one part of the process is the existence of fossils, particularly in the Short Woods and Hatch areas, where warm tropical seas ultimately led to the creation of limestone and coal, both of which were exploited in mining operations. Unfortunately, while these features were initially created as flat deposits whose subsequent weight compressed fine particles into hard rock, further geological activity caused splits, folds and other processes to alter their appearance and structure.

All this never-ending natural activity, coupled with man's interference and mineral exploitation, has led to the landscape we see today. In geological terms, the whole area comprising The Wrekin Hills is extremely complex and full of wonderful sites to explore. There are several disused quarries where features have been exposed as well as the ruins of a lime kiln, heavily overgrown but still with recognisable features.

There are also countless paths and tracks, some originating in pre-Roman times, which enable visitors to appreciate an intriguing array of scenes. Some have been made into discreetly signposted routes by Shropshire Wildlife Trust to reduce the likelihood of visitors getting lost or running the risk of personal injury, others have been left for independent adventurers to find their own way and, perhaps, discover something unique.

As a consequence, the few giants who may have had a hand in the development of the area no longer stroll around; they have been replaced by thousands of ramblers and day-trippers who are attracted here each year.

Even if they don't understand the geology, they do appreciate pleasant surroundings.

Southern view of the Forest Glen Pavilion (seen here, around 1915) built inside a former quarry on Lawrence Hill which also provided parking ground for vehicles, both horse-drawn and motorised. The main pathway up The Wrekin was directly opposite the front entrance to the Forest Glen. This postcard was produced for the Pavilion's then owner, Oswald Pointon.

South-west view of The Wrekin Hill as seen from the River Severn at Cressage, c. 1905.

Left and below: The Needle's Eye without the fallen rock, as seen from the west (1964) and east, *c.* 1900. Was the cleft formed by a giant's spade, or created at the very moment Christ died on the cross? Several myths surround the existence of the Needle's Eye. Cynics insist it was created by a natural weakness in the rock and that it lies on a geological fault line.

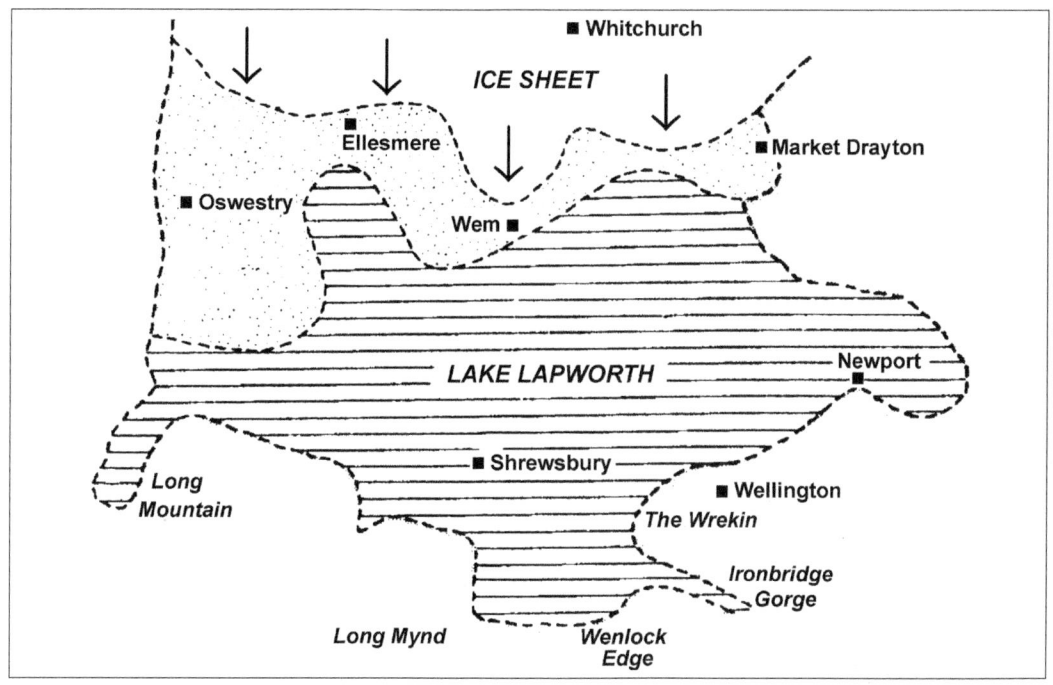

The extent of the conjectured glacial Lake Lapworth, which may have covered much of the Shropshire Plain when glaciers receded during the Ice Age. Mammoths and humans skirted around its shores in search of food. Rising water levels eventually overflowed, forming the Ironbridge Gorge, and redirected the flow of the river Severn southwards to the Bristol Channel; prior to the Ice Age, the river had joined the River Dee before flowing northwards into the Irish Sea.

Buildwas electricity generating power station was built on the river bank at the entrance to the Ironbridge Gorge in 1932; these large cooling towers were erected during the late 1960s. The view is from The Wrekin summit looking south, 2000. The reservoir in the centre is near Little Wenlock.

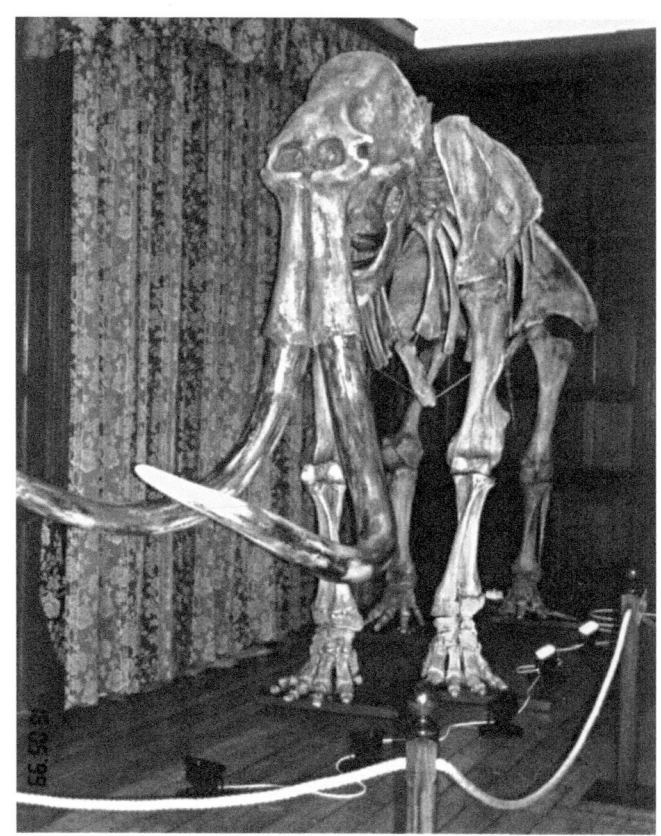

Left: The remarkably well preserved skeletons of a complete adult female (left) and three young mammoths were discovered at Norton Farm quarry near Condover, five miles west of The Wrekin, in 1986. They currently reside at Ludlow museum. It appears they all perished in a muddy pool, created when the ice retreated.

Below: The Cuckoo's Cup/Raven's Bowl being approached by Edwardian ladies, *c.* 1905.

three
Early Settlers

Very little is known for certain about the earliest inhabitants of The Wrekin Hill. There have only been two archaeological excavations in limited areas within the earthworks (in 1939 and 1973), plus one surface walk over in 2005. The 1939 excavation was intended to spread over two seasons but was curtailed by the onset of the Second World War, while the 1973 dig, which covered a very small area, was prompted by the imminent arrival of the television relay station on the northern face of the hill. The 2005 findings, sponsored by the Shropshire Hills Area of Outstanding Beauty, were essentially based on observations of surface features, the bulk of which shed light on activities from the Middle Ages onwards rather than the pre-Roman period. Sufficient evidence has been discovered to give some idea of who lived here and approximately when but further examination is required to clarify the situation.

Although there must have been Stone Age people living in the area from post-Ice Age times, evidence is sparse and takes the form of the occasional axe head; one was discovered on The Ercall during 1891. It appears that the original Wrekin fortress, the extent of which is uncertain, was created some 3,500 years ago. Its defences were rudimentary. Then, around 450 BC, new occupants arrived at the beginning of the Iron Age. The discovery of a large number of Bronze Age weapons by a farm worker digging drainage channels on Willowmoor in 1834 suggests a battle took place wherein the defenders lost. At some unascertained stage (whether pre-Iron Age or pre-Roman), the fortifications had fallen into decay and subsequent repairs were hastily made and show a lack of stone-building technique, thus indicating a long period of relative peace before the threat of attack re-emerged. The original fortress was either extended or contracted (archaeologists disagree) and strengthened, with alterations made to the outer embankments and entrances at Hell and Heaven Gates, although not at the south-western gate which, presumably, was little used because of the steepness and narrowness of the path beyond it.

The inner fort was littered with storage pits and timber-posted houses, many believed to be round in shape although the post holes make rectangular or square formations. Some had been

Aerial view of The Wrekin, believed to have been taken during the 1930s.

rebuilt following fire or general collapse (oak posts rot after about 100 years, thus indicating a period of occupation extending over several centuries). There is no proof that inhabitants lived here throughout the year; it is more likely that occupation was over winter or during periods of danger. Iron Age folk were essentially farmers, and no one in their right minds would live on top of a barren hill where water supplies were virtually non-existent. Excavations have produced many items including clay pots, a shale bracelet, a bronze-coated iron cow bell and a salt container from, unusually, the Droitwich area, all indicating a comfortable agricultural-based way of life.

Much speculation and wishful thinking has led to the belief that the Romans, when they arrived in the area in the late 40s AD, stormed the fortress. There is no conclusive evidence to support this claim nor, in fact, that a battle between the local Cornovian tribe and the invading army ever took place. The finding of a single javelin head on the hill and some evidence of burning timber does not make a battle. For more information on what may well have happened, see *Wrekin Wraiths, Rebels and Romans* by this author.

The Romans built a succession of forts at Wroxeter, a site some three miles away from The Wrekin and, after dismantling it around AD 80 when the occupying legion relocated to Chester, handed governorship of the settlement to leaders of the local Cornovian people. The town of Uriconium at Wroxeter rapidly developed into the fourth largest city in Roman Britain and it seems likely that the settlement on top of The Wrekin fell into disuse, the summit probably relegated to seasonal celebrations, perhaps with religious aspects.

More excavations are required to provide more tangible evidence of this period in The Wrekin's history. Whereas many hill tops in Shropshire bear evidence of Iron Age forts, The Wrekin seems to have been the most important. Why else would the Romans have built their legionary fortress nearby if the native population were greater elsewhere?

Early Bronze Age solid copper axe head found on The Wrekin in the nineteenth century.

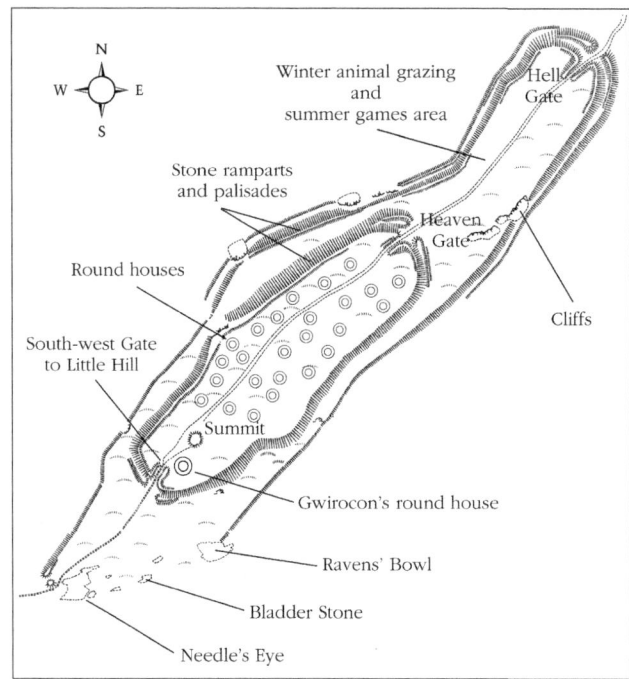

Left: Suggested plan of the Iron Age hill fort as shown in the novel *Wrekin Wraiths, Rebels and Romans* by this author. Druid king Gwirocon's round house gives a fictional clue as to how The Wrekin Hill may have acquired its name.

Below: Aerial view of the upper enclosure of the Iron Age hill fort in the 1940s, showing evidence of round houses near the wartime beacon atop the rocky outcrop in the centre. Heaven Gate lies to the bottom left of the picture while the south-western entrance is towards the top right.

August 1939 witnessed the first organised excavation of The Wrekin fort, sponsored by the Institute of Archaeology and supervised by Miss Kathleen Kenyon. A few volunteers chose to camp on the hill, others stayed in local hotels and travelled to the site on a daily basis. This was intended to be a preliminary exercise in preparation for full seasons of excavation during the next two years; the Second World War prevented any further activity.

Volunteer diggers explore the entrance to Heaven Gate and prepare the ground for subsequent excavation, August 1939.

Exposed guard room at the south-west entrance to the fort, August 1939. The area was backfilled after recording details to protect it from the elements and preserve it intact in case the area needed further examination by future archaeologists.

Volunteers at work during the 1973 excavations prior to the erection of the BBC television relay station on the northern face of the hill. The dig was supervised by S.C. Stanford.

four
Hill Economies

The next period in the human history of The Wrekin began during the Dark Ages when Anglo-Saxons settled in the area. Nearby Wellington began as a farmstead and developed into a small village. Thereafter, growth continued in the aftermath of the Norman Conquest and it was during the early Middle Ages that the modern town began to take shape. Economic and social growth depended on farming, which included exploitation of the woodland surrounding The Wrekin and it was probably during this period that the people of Wellington began to regard the hill as their own little mountain.

The Normans instituted a system of royal forests throughout the kingdom; although intended as areas reserved for the deer and boar hunting pleasures of kings and nobles and subject to harsh laws restricting their use by ordinary folk, the Royal Forest of The Wrekin, extending as it did from near Hadnall in the west to Shifnal in the east, provided somewhere for farm animals like pigs and cattle to graze (for a fee) as well as essential timber-based products like tools, fuel and accommodation. Charcoal burning began during these times and continued until the 1950s, and was especially important in the production of iron prior to the use of coke in the early eighteenth century.

The Wrekin also had a series of resident hermits who, tradition says, lived somewhere near the Burnt Cottage area of the hill. Before the activities of religious houses fell into disrepute, hermits were considered important enough to receive regular supplies of food from wealthy well wishers. The title 'Mount Gilbert' briefly assigned to The Wrekin was possibly named after one such hermit. Holy wells were frequently associated with remote places in medieval times: The Wrekin's was named after Saint 'Hawthorn' (perhaps a corruption of Alkmund); its location is not recorded but it was still curing skin diseases in the 1880s.

The royal forest effectively ceased to exist as a legal entity around 1300 but the woodland continued to be managed until the late twentieth century; the northern slopes in particular provided regular supplies of deciduous timber to R. Groom & Sons of Wellington for close on 100 years, and there is evidence of at least sixteen former saw pits scattered around the lower slopes. Steps are now being taken to revive some aspects of woodland management to counter years of neglect which, if allowed to continue, will cause lasting damage to the environment.

Between 1300 and the 1830s, fields were created from cleared woodland to enable greater use of the land for agricultural purposes; almost all of these fields were given names (as shown on tithe maps) and sometimes boundary stones were placed to show where one tract of land ended and another began. A few of them survive.

Ground level evidence of a small number of brick properties has been discovered all round the hill's base, including the Burnt Cottage remains; most were farmers', farm workers' and woodmen's cottages. Oddly, there are two Wrekin Farms, one to the north of the hill, the other to the south.

Whereas The Ercall and the other hills in the area have been severely exploited for their rocks and minerals for several centuries (most notably for house and road building materials and limestone), the archaeological walk-through in 2005 by Clwyd-Powis Archaeological Trust on behalf of Shropshire Hills Area of Outstanding Natural Beauty revealed the existence of about twenty pockets where quarrying had taken place long ago but the hill's main contribution to the local economy was a ready supply of timber.

One aspect of the hill's usage often overlooked is the existence of a rifle range which served various sections of the army for well over 100 years. Another is the BBC television relay station erected in the mid-1970s.

Ownership of The Wrekin Hill rests mainly with two landowning estates; the Orleton Estate, which tried to sell its holdings on the northern flank in 2004 amid public protests, and the Raby Estate which owns the majority of the remainder (including the summit, which has been designated as an ancient monument by English Heritage). Fortunately for the estimated 80,000 visitors to the hill annually, there are many long-established public rights of way.

Scene of R. Groom & Sons Timber Yard at Wellington, 1905. The road locomotive on the left was used to haul Wrekin logs on the eight-wheeled timber carriage on the right. At one time, the firm was the largest user of home-grown timber as well as the country's foremost foreign timber importer.

Lower section of the tree-lined main path up The Wrekin, around the 1910s, then quite narrow. Forest management (the coppicing and felling of trees to maintain a continuous source of good quality wood) was largely neglected during the latter half of the twentieth century. Action is now being taken to reverse the process to control growth and guarantee future supplies of healthy timber.

Willowmoor and the road leading from Little Wenlock to the Forest Glen, 2005. This area was once marshland and site of several Bronze Age burial mounds. It is believed the 'low' part of the name is derived from an Anglo-Saxon word meaning 'grave'. The land was levelled and drained for agricultural use during the 1830s. Note the roof of the Halfway House in the trees left of centre.

Damaged trees on the Little (Primrose) Hill stand alongside young firs, 2005.

Streams from The Wrekin area feed the reservoir to provide fresh water for the inhabitants of Wellington. First created during the latter half of the nineteenth century, it was subsequently enlarged. Folk have been known to fish here and skate on the ice during severe winters.

Aerial view looking north of the Halfway House (left) and the reservoir and Lawrence Hill quarry (right), June 2006. The cultivated land at the top formed Wrekin Common until the early nineteenth century, at which time it comprised light woodland and a few small fields.

Wendy Owen at the Burnt (known earlier as Lower) Cottage during an archaeological walk-through in 2005. The cottage is a reminder of the small number of properties built on the hillside, the rest of which have disappeared. Tradition says this is the site of a Wrekin hermitage in the Middle Ages.

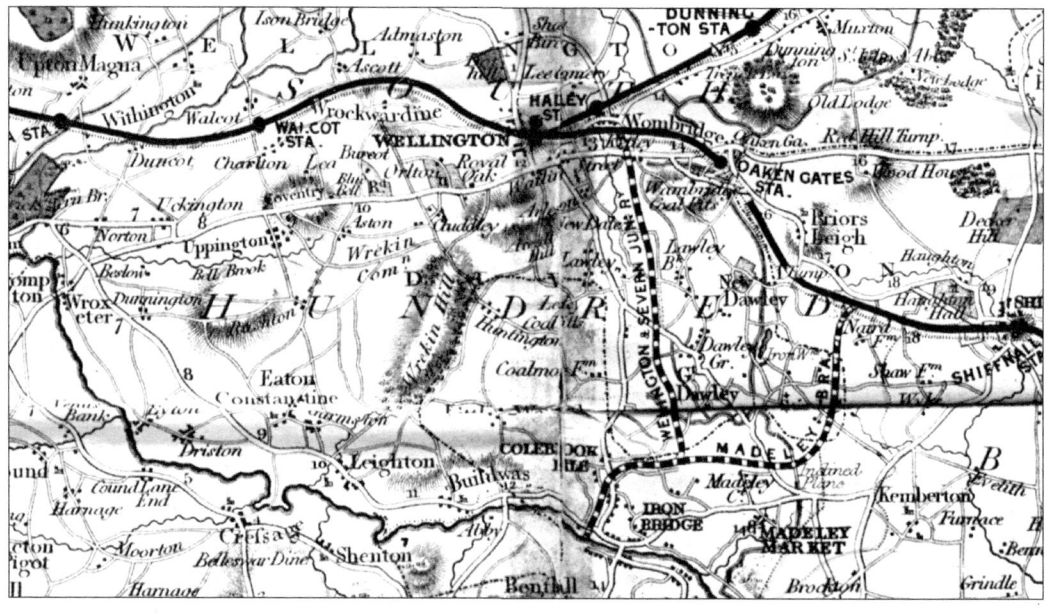

Extract from Crutchley's Railway Map of Shropshire, early 1850s, based on earlier Ordnance Surveys. Note 'Wrekin Common' mentioned to the north-west of The Wrekin. This area appears to have been the traditional name given to this part of the ancient Royal Forest of The Wrekin (or Mount Gilbert) assigned for use by local villagers who were allowed to graze their pigs, cattle and other livestock for a fee during the Middle Ages.

An archaeologist stands by a boundary stone, 2005. A few survive to mark the boundaries of small fields and other plots of land, some of which were subsequently supplemented by posts and wire fences. In some parts, banks of earthworks were also used to define ownership.

Ian Grant finds yet another charcoal platform, 2005; 126 were identified although there must have been considerably more scattered around the hillside. Many platforms, especially those at the north-east, were accompanied by embanked hollows where charcoal burners erected temporary shelters.

Above: Aerial view of The Wrekin from the south-west showing the current extent of woodland and cultivation, 2006.

Below: Outbreaks of fire can have devastating effects on woodland ecosystems. Fortunately, they are rare. A major conflagration took place in August 1989, when this fireman wearing a protective mask used a beater to extinguish smouldering grass. Tenders drove up and down the hill every fifteen minutes to replenish supplies of reservoir water until darkness called a halt to the proceedings.

Right: A soldier wiles away the time guarding a red warning flag on ground below Hell Gate while his comrades take part in shooting exercises on the Rifle Range at the foot of the hill's northern flank, 1967. The remnants of permanent warning signs are still to be found, although the range apparently ceased to be used during the 1980s after the MOD decided it was no longer required.

Below: The raised bank target area of the Rifle Range (which crossed the Wrekin Course road) lies towards the centre left of this photograph taken in 2002, after its numbered targets had been removed. A trench (littered with lead shot) ran along the back of the targets to allow a soldier to indicate with a raised flag whether a target had been hit. The range was already in use by local volunteers during the 1870s. Between then and its closure, members of the Territorial, Reservist and Regular armies as well as the Civilian Corps (1914-18) and the Home Guard (1940-44) made good use of the facility. Residents of Wellington always knew when practices were taking place as the sound of gunfire echoed around the town.

The Green Wood Centre (based at Coalbrookdale) arranged a guided tour for members of the public in January 2006. Its purpose was to explain why it is so important for woodland management techniques, including coppicing of deciduous trees, to be reintroduced to the hill.

The Wrekin gave its name to the medieval royal forest yet not many people realise there are still wild deer roaming around the woodland. Deer are shy animals, easily scared and have a tendency to flee silently whenever they sense danger. This rare proof of their continuing existence was taken by Andy Grundy, a Green Wood Centre woodsman, in February 2006.

five

Beacons and the BBC

Beacons made from burning timber have long been used as a means of communication in times of danger, spreading a warning along a chain of hill tops throughout the country. In more recent years, as in the case of Queen Elizabeth II's Silver Jubilee in 1977, they have been used for more celebratory purposes.

Perhaps the most endearing feature of The Wrekin Hill since the Second World War was the aircraft warning beacon, erected in 1942 after three British aircraft had crashed into the hillside. The beacon was operated remotely from RAF Shawbury using cables buried in the ground whose owners were approached by Barbers, estate agents of Wellington (the town's longest surviving firm) who negotiated access rights on behalf of the War Ministry. Its blinking red light acted as a sign of comfort and, since it could be seen from miles away, gave travellers returning to the area the reassurance that home was not far away. Furthermore, it became common practice in Wellington for children to say 'goodnight' to the flashing light from their bedroom windows.

The beacon was switched off at the end of 1964 as it was considered to be defunct. Subsequent public outcry led to questions being raised in Parliament, with the result that the light was acquired by the Wrekin Beacon Preservation Trust and switched back on for a few more years. Maintenance and running costs were, however, too high and the beacon was finally sold for scrap in 1970. Contrary to popular belief and wishful thinking, it was not re-erected at Sydney in Australia.

The loss of the pulsating red light was taken badly by many. However, the BBC needed a transmission booster station in Shropshire; The Wrekin Hill was chosen as a more suitable site than the Stiperstones, the only alternative offered. With the erection of the BBC television relay station in the mid-1970s, hopes were raised that a replacement light could be incorporated into its mast. It wasn't until the first minute of January 2000 that a flashing red light (albeit not so intense) returned to the hill, ostensibly as part of premature 'New Millennium' celebrations. A massive crowd assembled to witness the occasion.

---

7 November 1939: Airspeed Oxford P1845 crashed near the summit of The Wrekin Hill in bad visibility. Pilot P/O G.H.H. Coates killed, P/O W.O. Cramer severely injured.

27 July 1941: Bristol Beaufighter T3344 flew into The Wrekin in bad weather while on a training flight. This incident led to the beacon light being erected on The Wrekin. F/O O.B. Morrogh-Ryan and Sgt. H.R. Willis (AI operator) killed.

7 December 1941: Spitfire P7746 131 crashed into Little Hill by The Wrekin. 131 Squadron (based at Atcham) unable to land in a snow storm. Aircraft stalled, pilot bailed out at 150 feet but his parachute failed to open because of insufficient height. Sgt. H.A. Metcalfe killed.

17 December 1945: Airspeed Oxford LX530 21(P) aircraft crashed into The Wrekin.

12 September 1952: Avro Anson Mark T21 of the Central Navigation School at RAF Shawbury crashed in Wenlock Woods on The Wrekin. Pilot F/Sgt A.W. Gee died.

8 January 1994: Mooney M20J G-BSKJ aircraft flew into the Needle's Eye near The Wrekin summit. Melvyn Wroe and Harry Grocott were killed.

There were several other incidents between 1940 and 1944 where aircraft suffered mid-air collisions or hit overhead wires during low flying exercises but none seem to have actually flown into The Wrekin Hill itself. All wreckage appears to have been recovered at the time of each event.

List of aircraft which have crashed into The Wrekin since 1939.

Above and below: The Wrekin Beacon in 1958 and shortly before it was switched off, 1964.

Jim Bishop, seen here with a donkey and the 'swingle' boats at the Halfway House, was responsible for maintaining the beacon during the 1940s and 1950s.

R.G. Lawson (Wrekin Beacon Preservation Trust) receives the keys to the beacon cage from Squadron Leader F.T. Cooper (RAF Shawbury), 8 April 1965.

Sally Pilkington won the draw to switch the beacon light back on, 21 April 1965, after four months of darkness, at a barbecue and hillbilly event organised by the Wrekin Beacon Preservation Trust. Over 500 people attended.

A 'summit' meeting held in 1970 to determine precisely where the proposed television station should be sited. From left to right: G.J. Moon (BBC), C.J. Machin (Preservation of Rural England), Dr H.S. Bury (Wrekin Preservation Committee), N. Ingham (Salop Planning Department), John Dahl (Ministry of Housing inspector) and Bill Owen (Telford Chamber of Trade).

Above: After the battle to save it had been lost, volunteers help to dismantle the beacon, 28 August 1970. All that remained was its concrete base.

Below: Four years later, Midlands Electricity Board staff (from left to right) V. Evans, Phil Williams, Albert Woof and John Mannering lay power cables for the new transmitter.

Right: Wrekin Construction of Shifnal begins building work on the new television transmitting station, 1974. Because of the steep ascent and rough track, materials had to be brought from the foot of the hill to the site with tractors, trailers and dumper trucks.

Below: The transmitting station looking south, June 2006. Despite assurances that the 200ft mast would only be used for television signals, it is now festooned with devices for telephone and other radio communications. Representations from various concerned bodies meant that archaeological excavation work had to be carried out before construction began, and that the station must be built outside the northern boundary of the Iron Age fort, the rampart remnants of which can still be seen.

Above: An enormous crowd celebrates Queen Elizabeth II's Silver Jubilee at the beacon bonfire, June 1977.

Left: A brick cairn with a stainless steel toposcope (a diagram showing all places visible and their distances from the summit) was subsequently erected on the site of the Jubilee Beacon by Wellington Rotary Club and blessed by Sidney Austerbury, Archdeacon of Salop. From left to right: Gerry Powell (designer), Cyril Smith (Salop County Council Roads & Bridges Dept), Ray Hall (Rotary Club president and Wellington town councillor).

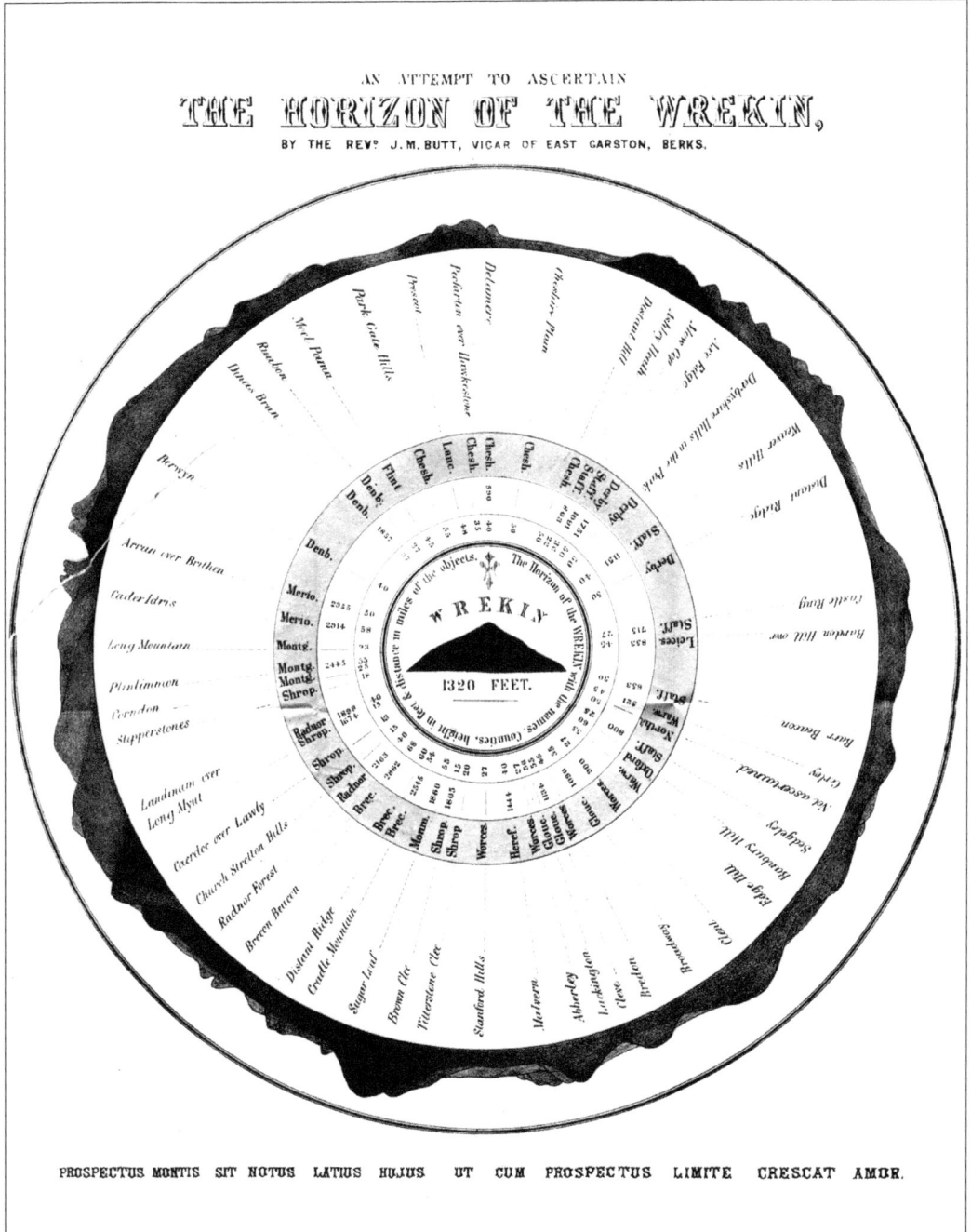

The stainless steel toposcope on top of the brick cairn was based on the drawing 'An Attempt to Ascertain the Horizon of The Wrekin' by Revd J.M. Butt, vicar of East Garston, Berkshire, in an 1870 guide to The Wrekin. The hill's biggest attraction to the new breed of Victorian tourist was its spectacular view from the summit and this particular illustration became the basis for further refinements as time went by and the concept of informative and useful guide books developed. Separate copies of the chart could also be bought for 1s.

Left: The steel plate on the toposcope cairn was replaced in 2005 by one donated by local firm Syspal as the original 1977 plate was showing signs of severe weathering. A large crowd assembled on the snow-capped summit for the unveiling, which coincided with the 100th birthday of the Rotary Club. As in 1977, Ray Hall presided over the affair. At the time, Ray said, 'As well as to commemorate 100 years of Rotary, this is dedicated to the life of Gerry Powell', the designer of the original plate who had recently died. From left to right: Syspal chairman Tony Roberjot, managing director Chris Truman, Wellington Rotary president Chris Goode and Ray Hall.

Below: As with the 1977 Silver Jubilee celebrations, another 'beacon bonfire' overnight party was held on the summit on 31 December 1999 to mark the arrival of the New Millennium, albeit a year early.

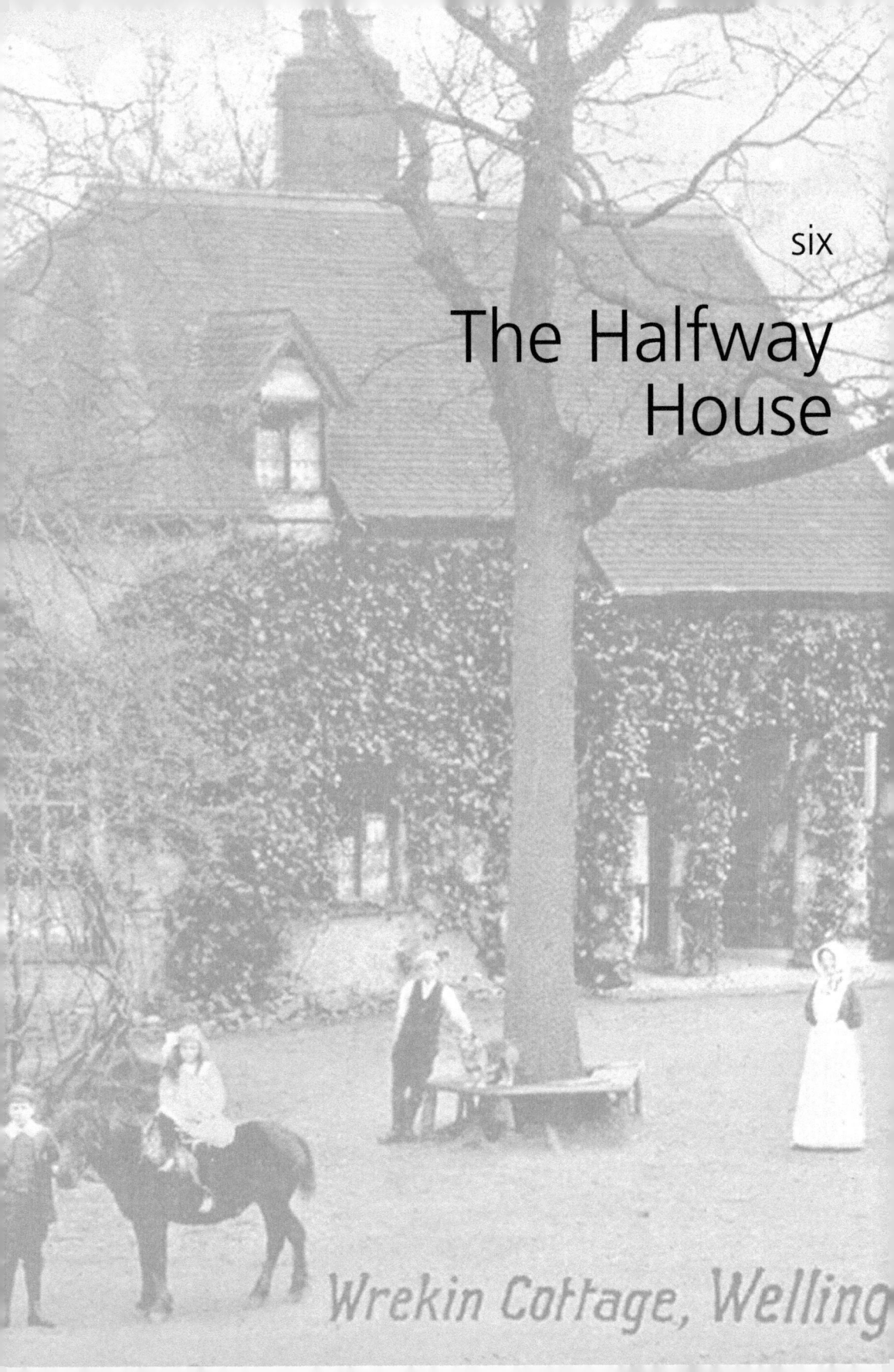

six

The Halfway House

Known as Wrekin Cottage and Upper Cottage at various times in its life, the Halfway House lies on the main pathway up The Wrekin. The present building was probably built originally during the late eighteenth century but may be on the site of an earlier structure or in an area exploited by temporary booths selling food and drink to revellers during the public holidays known as The Wrekin Wakes.

One of the earliest references to the cottage appears in a newspaper advertisement for a household effects auction held in 1851; even its 'famous Pelham tent' was sold afterwards at the Bull's Head hotel in Wellington. From this it would appear that the tent provided temporary enlarged accommodation for visitors than the small cottage could cater for. It also indicates that the tent had been used for a considerable amount of time.

The 1861 census shows farmer-cum-timber merchant Charles Jones living here, having leased the property after the death in 1858 of its previous occupant William Edwards, a woodsman, at the age of seventy-six. Charles's wife and daughter were stay makers and stitchers (stays were made for both men and women to keep them in shape) and he employed a dairy maid and a carter, implying that he had a few cattle and needed someone to take his varied products to market.

Thereafter, the cottage was occupied by the Birrell family. Adam was a game keeper, whose job was to ensure a regular supply of birds for shooting parties arranged by the Orleton Estate in the 1870s. He had a family of at least seven girls and at least one son. By all accounts, it was this family who did much to change the use of the house into an early type of café, catering for passers-by during the last quarter of the nineteenth century, when the arrival of railway services in Wellington led to a sharp rise in Victorian leisure pursuits, especially healthy ones which took place in the open-air.

By 1900, tea rooms, in competition with the Forest Glen at the foot of the hill, had gained a good reputation; their 'pavilion' was erected near the cottage to attract more visitors. A shed was used as an overflow facility, having previously been used as a storeroom and temporary stable. Farming activity gradually gave way to catering.

As time went by, son Arthur Birrell, Janet and other 'Miss Birrell' sisters ran the business. In 1937, S.C. Jones ran the Cottage Tea Rooms and was succeeded by 1950 by K.D. Walton. Richard Harper was proprietor from 1954 to 1962.

People can still remember the pavilion and shed being used to entertain children with a large display of photographs of famous film stars, posters and other cinema memorabilia until the late 1950s. The main attractions during the first half of the twentieth century until the 1960s were donkey rides and swing boats (known locally as 'swingle' boats).

Mr Lawson, then landlord of The Huntsman public house at nearby Little Wenlock, leased the property from the Orleton Estate in the 1960s; he introduced regular Saturday night dancing to music played by live bands in the pavilion. However, the cottage fell into considerable dilapidation during that period, which led to an effort to restore it to its former glory in 1969. It was a fairly short-lived exercise. Economic down-turns during the 1980s made it difficult to make a living as fewer folk visited the hill.

The present owners, Tom and Philomena ('Phil') Bolger, bought the cottage in October 1976 from Ken Jackson, who had purchased it from Vesey Holt (owner of the Orleton Estate) a few years earlier. Because of the economic situation in Britain for almost twenty years, Tom felt obliged to work abroad from the early 1980s and rented the cottage to Beverley Davidson, a classical musician.

The year 1998 marked Tom's return to the Halfway House. Since then, the surroundings have been tidied up considerably and the selling of refreshments to hill walkers reintroduced. Estimates put annual visitors to the hill during 2005 in the region of 80,000, which means they have a regular clientele each and every week, irrespective of the weather.

Right: Advertisement for the sale of household effects and livestock at the Upper Cottage, December 1858. John Barber conducted the sale; he was rapidly becoming a tremendous asset to the 'modernisation' of Wellington, partly because he had high values and was considered to be honest and trustworthy. In the early days of his business, many of John's clients included wealthy landowners. For more information concerning Wellington's oldest surviving business, see *The Story of Barbers, established 1848* by this author.

Below: Watercolour painting of the Upper Cottage, 1864.

SALE AT THE
UPPER COTTAGE, on the WREKIN.

MR. BARBER

Is instructed by the Representatives of the late Mr. William Edwards, to SELL BY AUCTION, on the above premises, on Tuesday next, the 14th day of December, 1858,

ALL the useful Out-door STOCK and Effects; comprising—3 superior in-calf Cows, capital Bay Pony, 7 years old, $13\frac{1}{2}$ hands high, steady in harness, and perfectly sound; Implements, Gearing, and Harness, Posts and Rails, &c.; also, the substantial Household FURNITURE, Feather Beds, Glass, Ware, Kitchen Requisites, and Dairy Vessels, and the far-famed PELHAM TENT, 36 feet long by 18 feet wide; also, a 2-Horse-power Vertical High-pressure STEAM ENGINE, with Boiler complete, &c.

Catalogues may be had at the Auctioneer's Office, Church-street, Wellington.

Sale to commence at Eleven o'clock precisely.

N.B.—The Pelham Tent will be erected on the Bull's-Head Inn Bowling Green, Wellington, and will be offered there after the above sale, at Six o'clock in the evening. The Engine may be seen by applying to Mr. CHARLES JONES, New-street, Wellington, any day before the sale.

Sketch of the Misses Birrell's Tea Rooms, Upper Cottage, drawn some considerable time before 1900. Note the absence of the Pavilion.

Possibly the earliest photograph taken of the Halfway House with the Pavilion, 1890s. The ladies in the centre are believed to be three of the Misses Birrell.

Wrekin Cottage Refreshment Rooms, early 1900s. The proprietor at this time was Arthur Birrell (thought to be standing by the horse), with two Misses Birrell nearby. A group of 'scholars' prepare to ride the donkeys, a popular feature for visitors.

Wrekin Cottage, early 1900s. An outdoor eating area with fixed bench picnic tables lies beyond the fence behind the young boy holding the donkey.

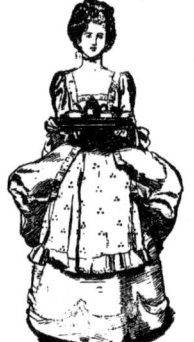

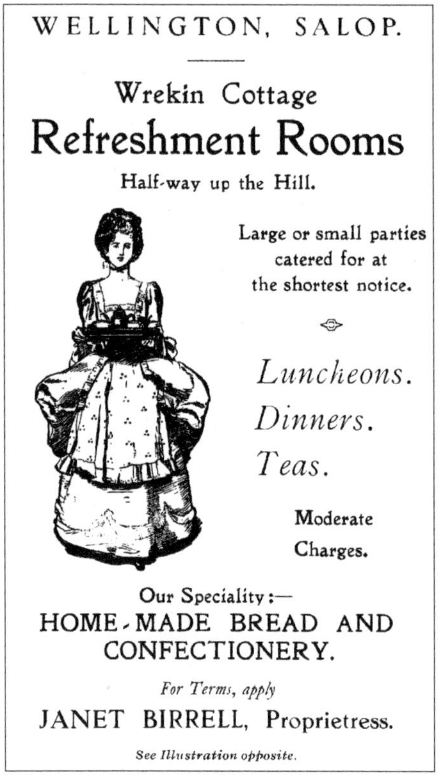
WELLINGTON, SALOP.
Wrekin Cottage
Refreshment Rooms
Half-way up the Hill.
Large or small parties
catered for at
the shortest notice.
Luncheons.
Dinners.
Teas.
Moderate
Charges.
Our Speciality :—
HOME-MADE BREAD AND
CONFECTIONERY.
For Terms, apply
JANET BIRRELL, Proprietress.
See Illustration opposite.

Left and below: Janet Birrell did much to raise the profile of the Wrekin Cottage during the years of and after the First World War. Locally produced town guides and directories provided an opportunity to advertise to a wider public, as did the popularity of sending holiday postcards showing scenes from places visited by tourists.

Opposite above: Although visits to the hill had been popular for decades, including annual Sunday school summer treats which entailed ferrying children from churches scattered around the district in horse-drawn wagonettes (some long distance journeys even involved travelling in canal tub boats), preferred customers were those willing to pay for meals and high teas. However, such customers expected more comfortable surroundings, which led to a sumptuous refurbishment of the dining room in the Pavilion, seen here in the 1920s.

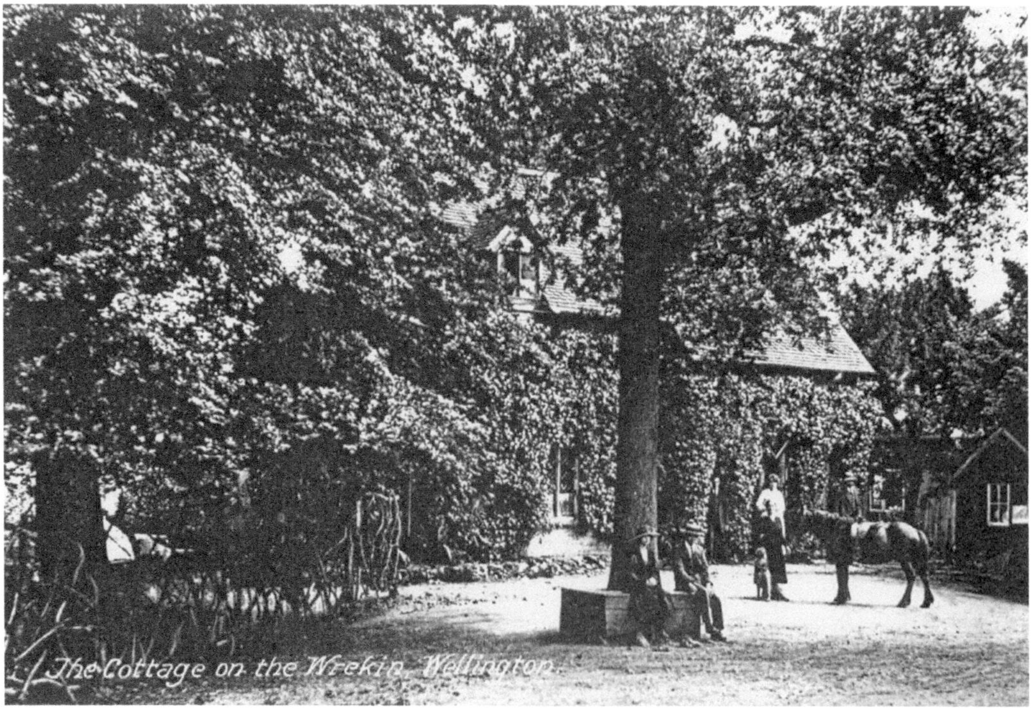
The Cottage on the Wrekin, Wellington.

Below: Wrekin Cottage, *c.* 1910. Although the main pathway up The Wrekin ran leftwards behind the hedge, visitors frequently took the slightly steeper route on the right.

Hobsons of Market Square, Wellington, produced this postcard (showing the opposite view of the steeper path shown previously), c. 1910. The Birrells kept their dog in the kennel away from the house to warn when people passed by at night.

'Swingle' boats (whose frame is visible in the centre of this postcard photograph) had been erected by the 1920s and gave an added incentive to spend time taking refreshments at the cottage.

Above and right: The swingle boats were a highly popular feature at the Halfway House for over forty years from the 1920s until the 1960s. Although intended for use by children, there was never any shortage of adults wanting to let their hair down. Although they had disappeared from the hill for many years, records show similar swing boats were already a regular feature during the Wrekin Wakes around 1800.

Left: William Bilboe (seen here with wife Ellen) travelled with Pat Collins' fair when it visited towns throughout the West Midlands. He also made sticks of rock for sale in Wellington market as well as at bank holiday stalls erected near the Halfway House in the 1920s. William's sons also tended the donkeys and the swingle boats.

Below: From about 1900 until the 1930s, A.E. Bourne's Fine Art & Fancy Bazaar in New Street, Wellington, commissioned a wide range of porcelain and other souvenirs for visitors to the hill. This cup and saucer features scenes from The Wrekin. All the pictures were adapted from popular postcards of the day.

Right: Efforts are made to spruce up the appearance of the Halfway House, 1969, when Mr Lawson, landlord of The Huntsman in Little Wenlock, rented the property from the Orleton Estate.

Below: The Wrekin Hill, looking north-west, June 2006. The Halfway House clearing in the woodland is seen towards bottom right. Once an initial bend has been negotiated above the cottage, the remainder of the pathway to the summit is almost straight. Fields at Willowmoor lie bottom centre.

The bend in the pathway above the Halfway House, 1920s.

Aerial view of the Halfway House as seen from the east, June 2006.

Tom and Phil Bolger at the columned entrance to their Halfway House, October 2006. They have done a remarkable job in reviving the sale of refreshments to hill walkers since their return to the cottage in 1998.

Author Allan Frost (left) and Tom at the first ever book signing on The Wrekin, Sunday 29 October 2006. Allan's novel *Wrekin Wraiths, Rebels and Romans* is a thrilling adventure which begins with two people squeezing through the Needle's Eye, only to find themselves transported back 2,000 years where they become involved in the war between the invading Roman army and the first real British hero, King Caradoc. This present book, *The Wreckin Hill*, was launched here in April 2007 and is the first book ever to be launched on the hill.

Left: Ross and Tot Vickers buy welcome refreshment at the Halfway House, 2006. Ross is chairman of the Wellington Civic Society. The building to the right is the small toilet block for use by visitors.

Below: The Halfway House as it is today. In contrast to earlier photographs, Tom has built a fence across the entrance to the cottage in order to preserve domestic privacy at times when the refreshments area (which is festooned with rustic seats made by Tom from tree trunks) is closed.

seven
The Forest Glen

The narrow valley between The Wrekin and Lawrence Hill is known as the Forest Glen. Nowadays the road to Little Wenlock runs along the valley floor. Although there must have been a woodland track here from prehistoric times, tradition has it that the first significant road was created in 1102 by King Henry I to shorten the march of his army to Bridgnorth. Much of Shropshire had been put under Roger de Montgomery's charge by William I, a blood relative, after the Norman Conquest but Roger's son Robert rebelled against Henry I and fortified the castle at Bridgnorth. The rebellion was crushed and the de Montgomery lands in Shropshire and Wales were divided among the king's supporters.

Why Lawrence Hill is so named is not known; it may refer to a farmer or the church of St Lawrence at Little Wenlock, in whose parish the hill lies; in fact, it is shown as St Lawrence Hill on some, but not all, old maps. The part of the valley nearest the reservoir, constructed in the latter half of the nineteenth century and fed by streams to provide clean water to the inhabitants of Wellington, was prone to flooding after heavy rain until the early 1890s when corrective measures were taken. On the other hand, Ercall Lane, the road leading to Buckatree Hall (so called, legend has it, because a deer leapt into a tree to escape dogs while being hunted) was, until well into the 1960s, regularly littered with the bodies of countless frogs, crushed beneath the tyres of passing cars. They should have had more sense than to leave the safety of the reservoir.

Whereas The Wrekin had been a playground for local folk for centuries, it wasn't until the inauguration of railway services to Wellington in 1849 that the hill became an immensely popular venue for tourists, many of whom stayed in the town's hotels and hired horses, traps and bicycles to take them to the Forest Glen, the starting point for a leisurely, occasionally strenuous, walk to the summit. Some took picnic baskets but a great many didn't. It soon became apparent that here was a wonderful business opportunity for someone willing to provide refreshments and a monitored parking area for horses, bicycles and other vehicles at the foot of The Wrekin.

Henry William Pointon, a Freemason, ran the Station Hotel in Wellington and the Red Lion Hotel on Holyhead Road. Comments from visitors inspired him to build the Forest Glen Pavilion in a corner of a quarry on Lawrence Hill in 1889. (The quarry continued to be worked on a small scale until the mid-1920s.) He leased the plot from Lord Forester. The enterprise was an immediate success. As time went by, the Pavilion became an authorised venue for members of the Cyclists Touring Club (CTC) and a highly esteemed establishment catering for busloads of tourists, particularly at weekends and Bank Holidays, in addition to casual visitors. Furthermore, Sunday schools in the district ferried children there in wagonettes as a 'treat' in summer months and played games on the hill before returning to the Pavilion for tea and sandwiches.

Apart from a short period, all catering was done by the Pointons themselves and their employees. In fact, their ability to serve satisfactory meals to substantial numbers of guests led to the introduction of wedding receptions and dinner dances, the latter being arranged over the Christmas period for businesses employing large numbers of staff, clubs and societies at all times of the year, and for the enjoyment of anyone who turned up on a Saturday night. Many folk can still remember eating a meal under the watchful eyes of stuffed wild animals and birds; it could be a little disconcerting to see 'Wrekin Fox' on the menu when one of the stuffed animals might well have been a relative.

Rooms were heated in winter by paraffin heaters, removed shortly before visitors arrived. Sanitary facilities consisted of chemical toilets (requiring regular visits from the 'soil cart') until a cesspit was dug next to, of all places, the reservoir in the 1940s. Even then, visiting the gents presented additional problems as the pipework had a tendency to spout leaks from the joints.

It was the morning after an American farewell dance in September 1943 that the partly clothed body of Private Louisa Jenny Price, an eighteen-year-old ATS. girl from Birkenhead, was found in nearby undergrowth. Her head had been smashed. Sergeant Michael Pihosh of the American army was charged with murder because his trousers were unaccountably spattered with blood. He was

Visionary partners: Henry William Pointon (1836-1908) with his second wife Sarah Ann Millward (1845-1905) whom he married in 1867, as seen in the 1890s. Henry apparently had five children by first wife Mary Paddock (1838-1866) and a further thirteen by Sarah, the last being in 1887 ... yet they still found time to run the Station Hotel in Wellington and the Red Lion public house on Holyhead Road as well as the Forest Glen Pavilion.

tried at a court martial held in an American camp in the West Midlands and was acquitted on the strength of him losing all recollection of events that night because he'd been on a prolonged pub crawl in Wellington and continued drinking heavily at the Forest Glen afterwards, coupled with conflicting eye witness accounts from his comrades. American authorities promised to continue enquiries but nothing further transpired except that Pihosh was returned quietly to America.

Henry Pointon died aged seventy-three in 1908, whereupon the business passed to his son Oswald, who continued Henry's tradition of reciting the ancient toast 'To All Friends Round The Wrekin' to guests at the Station Hotel and, shortly afterwards, at events held in the Pavilion. By all accounts, 'Ossie' was quite a character. Nothing was too much trouble for him, not even when he served dinner to a party of guests at the summit of the hill, a feat which entailed him making countless journeys to and from the Pavilion during the course of a single evening. Business expanded so much that an extension and separate bungalow (for Ossie's occupation) had to be added to the Pavilion in 1918.

Ossie died, aged eighty-three, in 1956, whereupon his son Percy inherited the business. Joyce Pitchford, niece of Percy's late wife, took it over after his death in 1978 and ran it with her husband Don. Things were never the same. Visitor numbers had fallen considerably in recent years and the buildings required substantial renovation. The Pitchfords erected another extension at the front of the main Pavilion in an effort to attract more business but the District of The Wrekin Council refused to grant retrospective planning permission. A disastrous fire almost destroyed the Pavilion shortly afterwards and dereliction followed. The buildings were demolished in 1990.

The Ironbridge Gorge Museum collected the remains and began the slow process of restoration. Marjorie McCrea, Henry Pointon's granddaughter, attended a ceremony in 1993 when the Duke of Kent laid a new foundation stone at Blist's Hill Museum, and visited the site again on 24 May 1994 when the newly restored Forest Glen Pavilion was officially opened to the public by Adele Biss of the English Tourist Board and the British Tourist Authority.

The site of the former Forest Glen Pavilion was acquired in 2005 by Shropshire Wildlife Trust with money raised from a public appeal. The area was subsequently tidied up and now provides car parking facilities for thousands of visitors each year. Hopefully, a permanent visitor centre, complete with refreshments and toilets, will be built on the site to act as a suitable and worthwhile replacement for such an essential amenity.

In the meantime, visitors have to purchase refreshments from the Halfway House. And, perhaps, one day, the public conveniences erected several years ago by the local borough council will be open for use.

Lawrence Hill quarry around 1910. This was a long-established popular venue for picnics, a fact which influenced Henry Pointon's choice for his site for the Forest Glen Pavilion.

A Hobsons (printers of Wellington) drawing of the Forest Glen Pavilion produced shortly after its opening in 1889.

Above: Horse-drawn transport was commonplace from the 1890s until the late 1920s.

Below: Henry Pointon (centre) takes advantage of the growing number of Cyclist Touring Club (CTC) members seeking suitable stopping off places for refreshment in the late 1890s. The poster on the gate post warns visitors not to steal the rhododendrons. Stabling for visitors' horses was provided in the building on the far right.

Above and below: Before 1910 the Pavilion comprised a single building. Growing numbers of visitors both during and after the First World War led to the construction of a small cottage to the left in which Ossie Pointon and his growing number of catering servants lived for a while. Eventually supplies were stored here and further conversion enabled it to be used as an overspill facility for large gatherings. The main path up The Wrekin is through the gateway on the right.

Above: By the 1920s, the advent of charabanc buses enabled greater numbers of visitors to travel to The Wrekin from all over the district on Bank and other public holidays. This period also marked an increase in private car ownership which continues to bring folk to the hill on a daily basis.

Below: The Forest Glen Pavilion, 1930s. Trellises added rustic charm to the appearance of the buildings. The words 'Refreshment Pavilion' had been removed from the roof when it was re-roofed, *c.* 1920.

Forest Glen Pavilions

FOOT OF WREKIN

These Pavilions have been noted for 40 years for

LUNCHEONS, DINNERS and TEAS for PICNIC
and COACH PARTIES, MOTOR and CYCLING
CLUBS, BIRTHDAYS, WEDDINGS
COMINGS of AGE, DANCES
WHIST DRIVES

Makes an Ideal centre for a day's outing—1,320 ft. above sea level. Ramble over the Glorious Wrekin, beautiful walks and drives, and wonderful views of 17 Counties.

VISIT the NEEDLE'S EYE and CUCKOO'S CUP

MAKE A DAY OF IT AT THE WREKIN!

The Forest Glen Pavilions cater for you.   Open Daily
ROOMS for 500.   PIANO.   GARAGE

Phone 363   **J. O. POINTON, WELLINGTON, Salop**

THE FOREST GLEN PAVILION

THE FOREST GLEN — THE WREKIN

One of Shropshire's Famous Beauty Spots

An Ideal Centre for

Your Spring and Summer Outings

or

WEDDING RECEPTIONS AND
EVENING PARTIES

THE WREKIN, Near WELLINGTON

Telephone: WELLINGTON 3332

The Wrekin Toast

*To all friends round The Wrekin
and, to her most loyal Majesty, the loyalty she is seeking.*

To Shropshire's sons upon the sea
   On land and in the air,
There never were, nor ever will
   Be finer anywhere.

For they have never bowed the knee
   In bondage to a foe.
Nor ever will, while they have breath,
   To fight as best they know.

And may the good Lord please rain down
   Upon our foe's bare shins
As many Holy pebble stones
   As they've committed sins.

In order that we'll know them
   By the way they cringe and crimp
But more especially so we'll know
   The b*ggers by their limp!

This ancient toast, which has varied slightly over the centuries, was immortalised by renditions given to unsuspecting visitors by Henry, Ossie and Percy Pointon. The toast is known to have existed for more than 300 years. George Farquhar dedicated his play *The Recruiting Officer* (an English Civil War comedy set in Shrewsbury) to 'All friends round The Wrekin' when it was first performed in 1706; even then, the toast was long established and well known throughout the country.

Above: By the 1940s, family trips to The Wrekin with the prospect of an ice cream or high tea at the Forest Glen Pavilion had become a regular occurrence at weekends as well as public holidays. The Midland Red and other local bus companies periodically laid on regular short term services which ran to and from Wellington to swell visitor numbers.

Opposite, above and below: Very few advertisements were placed for the Forest Glen Pavilion in town or county guides. Times change, so the 1930s advertisement was intended for a different type of clientele than that appearing in a 1960s *Urban District Official Guide for Wellington*, Shropshire.

Above and below: Private parties for weddings, birthdays and so on, were a regular occurrence throughout the Forest Glen Pavilion's existence. One of the first was for the Pointon family and important Wellington business associates, *c.* 1900. Oakengates pensioners benefited from annual visits provided free of charge by local small bus operators during the 1950s.

Above: Christmas dinner dance at the Forest Glen for Barber & Son staff at Wellington, Dawley and Market Drayton offices, 1960s. Dinner dances and parties for office and works staff from businesses and members of various organisations throughout the district were a regular event, especially during the run up to and shortly after Christmas.

Below: Wellington Ladies' Circle enjoys a 'cowboys and Indians' themed dinner dance in 1961.

The Pavilion's final days. An auction held by Barbers of Wellington disposes of the contents, which included stuffed creatures and a staggering amount of rare Coalport china, 1979.

One of the last photographs taken of the premises shows later additions, like the unauthorised extension on the right, mid-1980s. A fire almost destroyed the buildings completely.

The President, Chairman and Members
of the
IRONBRIDGE GORGE MUSEUM TRUST
have pleasure in inviting

Miss M. McCrea

to the visit of
His Royal Highness The Duke of Kent
to lay the foundation stone of the Forest Glen Pavilion at Blists Hill
and to launch Industrial Heritage Year in the Heart of England

on Wednesday 17 March 1993 at 12 noon

R.S.V.P. by Friday 12 March 1993

Above and right: Marjorie McCrea, eighty-five-year-old granddaughter of Henry Pointon, was a special guest at Blist's Hill Open Air Museum when the foundation stone (bearing Henry's initials) was laid by HRH The Duke of Kent in March 1993 in preparation for erecting the newly restored Pavilion. Marjorie's mother, Louisa Pointon, had managed the original Pavilion for a short time before 1903 when she married John McCrea. At that time, the Pavilion was open from Easter until September. By the 1920s, months of opening were extended in response to growing demand and party bookings. Sadly, Marjorie passed away on 30 November 2006.

The restored Forest Glen Pavilion at Blist's Hill Museum, complete with the original 'Refreshment Pavilion' roof lettering, was officially opened on 24 May 1994. The ceremony, again attended by special guest Marjorie McCrea, was performed jointly by the English Tourist Board and British Tourist Authority.

Above and below: The Forest Glen Pavilion site was purchased following a public appeal led by Shropshire Wildlife Trust. Decades-old graffiti painted on the Lawrence Hill quarry cliffs was removed by the environmental cleaning firm G-Force in February 2006 before the ground was converted the following month into a visitor car park.

eight

People's Playground and Paraphernalia

The Wrekin Hill is one of the most distinctive and recognisable landscape features in Shropshire. Visitors have flocked to its slopes for centuries, attracted by its clean air and superb views. It wasn't always so.

Historically, people don't tend to climb a hill just because it's there; they have to have a reason. The Wrekin hasn't been used as a place of refuge for some 2,000 years, and warning beacons are something of a rarity. Entertainment for ordinary folk was not an every day occurrence until relatively recent times. Until the latter half of the twentieth century, people had little spare time to pursue leisure activities; they worked long hours and were paid a pittance. Fun was something so rare that it had to be enjoyed to the full on those occasions when the opportunity arose.

The earliest records of hill-inspired 'fun' relate to the battles which took place between the farmers and apprentices of Wellington and colliers from the neighbourhood. They were held annually during the Wrekin Wakes in May (and occasionally June – exact dates varied) and the object of the exercise was to keep possession of the summit. The fighting was fierce: tradition says that fatalities were accepted as a natural hazard. If the sides were evenly balanced, messengers were despatched to outlying villages to muster support. Events got so out of hand during the 1740s that the local militia were called out, the Riot Act read and several people were arrested for breach of the peace.

The Wakes continued, as did the fighting, but here was so much drunkenness and licentiousness that local magistrates banned the custom, probably during the 1840s. Around 1800, a resident of Wellington wrote:

> The top of the old hill was covered with a multitude of pleasure-seekers, with ale-booths, ginger-bread standings, gaming tables, swing boats, merry-go-rounds, three-sticks-a-penny, and all the etceteras of an old English fair.

Things hadn't changed much 100 years later, when Col. E.W. Herbert of Orleton commented on the nuisance caused by, 'trippers & cocoa-nut people who put up stands and make a horrid mess.'

The Wrekin was visited at other times of the year for a variety of reasons. Sunday school children were ferried there as an annual 'treat' in a wide range of vehicles (including, in July 1883, traction engines (two engines and eight trucks) belonging to Ketley Iron Works. People held tea parties and family reunions at the summit; individuals as well as societies came to explore the woodland walks and examine the abundant flora and fauna. More and more visitors came from outside the area on trains and, later, buses and motor cars. It was during the late Victorian period that the phrase, 'Going round the Wrekin to get to Wellington' was coined, meaning a long detour or a long-winded way of explaining something.

As is so often the case with tourists, they desired a souvenir of their visit. Guide books, maps, postcards and an assortment of cheap souvenirs appeared on the scene during the 1870s. The earliest mass-produced postcards date from the 1890s. They were cheap to buy and, in an age when cameras were not widely owned, gave a photographic image to jog the memory for many years afterwards. It was not long before other souvenirs, particularly porcelain vases, cups, saucers and trinket trays, found their way into Wellington's shops.

The Wrekin was adopted as a symbol for other products apparently associated with healthy living: beer, fizzy pop in various flavours and even tobacco. Because of the hill's significance and reputation, businesses adopted its name: the Wrekin Hotel in Market Square, Wellington, was one of the first to do so as a means of attracting custom from increasing numbers of visitors. Many businesses continue to include 'Wrekin' in their trading names.

People still flock to the hill in their thousands to explore its secrets, picnic or see its views. Depending on the weather, they mountain bike, ski, toboggan, hang glide, paraglide (someone recently took off at the summit and landed at Stonehenge, some 140 miles away!), horse ride, fell run (seventeen minutes from bottom to top and back again), scout camp, walk for charity ... or simply walk, with or without their dogs.

The Wrekin Hill has so much to offer.

WELLINGTON RACES

ON Monday the 14th of September, 1761, will be run on the Wreken Course, a match for FIFTY POUNDS, between Mr. Corbett's Bay Gelding *Jack come tickle me;* and Mr. Dixon's Brown Mare, *Northern Nancy.*

And, on Tuesday, the Day following, will be Run for on the same Course, A Purse of FIFTY POUNDS, by any Horse, Mare, or Gelding, that never started for the above the value of Five Pounds. Four Years old Horses to carry 9ft. and aged 10ft; each horse to be shewn and entered at the Town-Hall in Wellington, on Saturday the 12th of September, between the Hours of 1 and 6 in the Afternoon; each to pay 5s Entrance, or double at the Place of Starting. – To be subject to Articles. – Three to start or no race. N.B. No Person will be permitted to erect Booths upon the said Course, or sell any Liquor, but what are subscribers to the Purse. – There will be good Ordinaries each Day at the Talbot, Red Lion, and Pheasant Inns.

Newspaper advertising a gentlemen's horse race, 1761. The Wrekin Course is the long straight road running parallel to The Wrekin on its northern side. Judging from the note at the end, impromptu appearances of stall holders at public events presented problems for the organisers, especially if they sold gin, the nation's most popular beverage after beer. In addition to racing, fox hunting was also a popular pastime for those who could afford it. Furthermore, a 1758 directory of Shropshire states an area belonging to Brook Forrester was well stocked with deer, presumably another opportunity for hunting where the kill could actually be eaten.

The Wrekin's fame was known countrywide as this token produced for the festival to celebrate the return of the Conservative members for Shropshire, 1842, confirms. The obverse side (left) shows The Wrekin Hill in the distance behind Shrewsbury Abbey and the English Bridge.

A View of The Wrekin Hill painted by Chatelaine in 1758.

View over Wellington towards The Wrekin drawn as a lithograph by W. Gauci for the *Shropshire Gazetteer* published by T. Gregory, *c.* 1800.

A 1920s postcard published by Keay of Wellington showing a view of The Wrekin over the town's then Recreation Ground. Postcards were regarded as affordable miniature works of art.

Opposite below: The Wrekin from Leighton published by W. Emans of Birmingham, *c.* 1820.

Above: A visit to The Wrekin by the Severn Valley Field Club as portrayed in an *Illustrated London News* article of 1873. On the left members forage in the woods. On the right is a view of the hill. The club was formed in the 1860s to provide leisure pursuits for those who had time on their hands. Railway trains enabled them to travel relatively long distances, often involving overnight stays in suitable hotels and the hiring of horses and traps to their chosen site.

Below: Illustrations of the hill were still comparatively rare when this drawing of The Wrekin Hill from Charlton was published in *Our Own Country* magazine in the 1880s.

Above and below: Wellington Railway Station and Henry Pointon's Station Hotel, 1890s. Visitors could stay at the hotel and hire horses and traps (with or without a driver) to take them to The Wrekin from various establishments in the town, most particularly the Ercall Hotel in Market Street.

An early 1880s drawing of Ercall Lane (sometimes called Wrekin Drive), the main route from Wellington to the foot of the hill.

The same stretch of road seen in an early postcard photograph.

Right: Early maps, especially those bound into books, were too large for travellers to carry easily, so 'ribbon' maps, confining detail to those places on either side of the recommended route, provided a handy alternative. This one was produced by Daniel Paterson in 1785. The Wrekin is clearly shown, as is the Royal Oak, the nearest coaching station to the hill offering overnight accommodation and a change of horses. The Royal Oak had previously been a farmhouse and later became the Falcon Inn. It is now the Old Orleton restaurant.

Below: Facsimile copy of *Handbook to The Wrekin*, first published in 1895. Guides like this (which incorporated the toposcope chart devised by Revd J.M. Butt) were very popular as they provided a wealth of (often inaccurate) information regarding the geography, history, flora and fauna of the hill as well as promoting other attractions in the vicinity, such as Uriconium Roman City, Lilleshall and Buildwas Abbeys and the Priory at Much Wenlock.

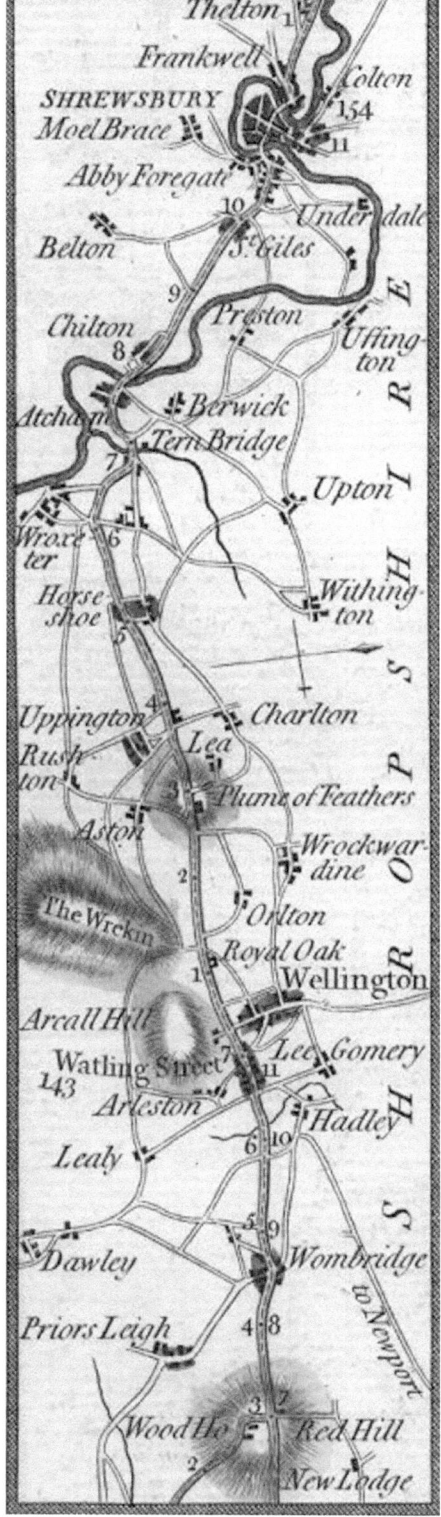

It is not often that I have to tell of a snake being found hereabouts, and so I think I may as well give publicity to a statement which a gentleman made to me the other day, to the effect that sauntering aimlessly up The Wrekin on Saturday last, he was somewhat surprised when nearing the summit to see the ferns, some yards in front of him, considerably agitated. Thinking that the agitation was caused by a rabbit or some other denizen of the hillside, he hurried to the place, when he was surprised to see a snake, several feet long, glide out of the undergrowth and ascend a neighbouring tree, making a peculiar hissing sound the while. Upon examining the place from whence it had proceeded, he was further astonished to find portions of a rabbit covered with the saliva of the snake, evidently preparatory to mastication, with other signs that he had disturbed the reptile at its meal. My informant approached the tree, on a branch of which the snake was lying, and had a good opportunity of examining it. He sends me the particulars of the dimensions and general appearance of the reptile, which I have forwarded to a friend skilled in the identification of strange specimens; but I have not yet heard that he has been successful in classifying the snake. However, it may interest the reader to know it must have been nearly six feet in length, and that when approached too nearly it showed no signs of fear, but reared its head and continued to hiss in a manner somewhat similar to a steam engine. On other people approaching, however, it retreated into the woods at a pace that baffled all pursuit.

Above: Odd happenings on and around The Wrekin were diligently reported in local newspapers. This article appeared in an 1889 edition of the *Wellington Standard*, whose editor frequently adopted a tongue-in-cheek approach to suspect newsworthy items.

Left: The Wrekin Hotel, Market Square, Wellington, *c.* 1890s. The hotel chose its name to appeal to the rising number of tourists wishing to visit The Wrekin Hill. It was only a two-minute amble from the railway station and advertised itself as a temperance hotel for a while in order to appeal to family groups and abstainers. It had the opposite effect, so the hotel abandoned the idea and reinstated 'normal' alcohol availability. The Wrekin Hotel, in common with other establishments without stabling facilities, had an arrangement with the Pierces who ran the Ercall Hotel some 150yds down Market Street, the road to the right.

Right and centre right: A decorated tea pot and saucer and two souvenir vases featuring The Wrekin and Halfway House, made around 1920 specifically for A.E. Bourne's gift emporium in Wellington.

Centre left and bottom: An exquisite Coalport plate and two Coalport cups. Unfortunately the cup on the left includes a castle (The Wrekin does not have a castle). Coalport produced high quality chinaware for discerning visitors. A.E. Bourne was content to serve the less discerning masses.

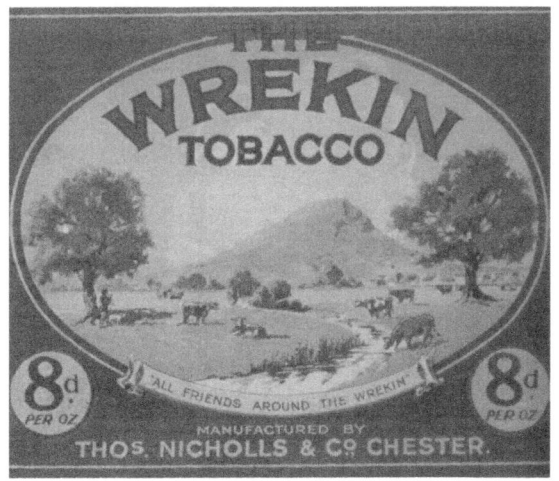 

Above, left and right: Use of The Wrekin's name in promoting 'healthy' products included a tobacco tin in the 1920s and a Wrekin Ales yellow ashtray from the 1940s. The ashtray and other Wrekin Brewery Old Foley advertising porcelain was manufactured by James Kent Ltd, Staffordshire.

Up The Wrekin before Sunrise
New Street Methodist Youth Club, Wellington (Salop), has a reputation for doing strange things. So anyone who heard twenty-four young people creeping through the streets at three o'clock one Sunday morning recently probably surmised that 'New Street' was up to something again!

The object of this middle-of-the-night exodus was to reach the top of The Wrekin (1335 feet and two miles distant) in time to see the sun rise. Its organisers were so determined to get the party to the summit in time that they actually reached it nearly an hour too early! But it was a perfect morning and a sunrise worth waiting for. 'Better the day, better the deed,' they said.

Above left: Climbing The Wrekin to watch the sun rise on Midsummer's Day is a long tradition, both for individuals and members of a group such as the New Street Methodist Youth Club in Wellington, which maintained the annual pilgrimage for many years from the time it began in 1947.

Above right: Freemasons held regular ladies' festivals (or evenings) at the Forest Glen. Programmes were printed for each occasion (such as this one in 1946) and provided a source of amusement as attendees attempted to obtain the signatures of everyone present.

Elizabeth Pierce (fourth from the right) of the Ercall Hotel in Wellington not only hired vehicles for visitors to go to The Wrekin. She and her family enjoyed a picnic together in 1922.

The Wrekin summit is an odd yet somehow appropriate choice for family get-togethers. Four generations of Evans's meet at the toposcope cairn, 2001. From left to right, back row: Joolie, Mark, George, Lucia ('Luby'), Mia, Paul and Steve. Front row: Deanne, Jayne, Nancy.

Above left: Caroline and Tim Frost take a break between toboggan rides down the hill towards the bend in the pathway above the Halfway House, 1979. The Ercall is in the distance.

Above right: There have been many unusual races up and down the hill over the years, like this barrel race for charity in 2005. Competing teams struggled to carry a 9gal firkin weighing 50kg. Winners for the sixth time in seven years (taking twenty-three minutes two seconds) were the Cock Hotel Hobsons Harriers. Winners of the empty barrel race were women of the Wrekin Angels team.

A BBC outside broadcast van broke down in January 1967 and had to be towed by a local breakdown lorry. The television team was on its way to the top to establish a TV link between Wrexham and Manchester for a boxing programme scheduled for transmission that afternoon.

Scouts keep warm around the fire at their 'log settlement' on the south-west slope of the hill, 1920s. The Scout camp has provided countless weekends and overnight stays for scout and guide groups ever since. Note the totem pole just right of centre.

The last Wrekin Run is about to start, May 2006. This annual race from the Orleton Park (formerly Wellington Modern) school to The Wrekin summit and back was a tradition which began in 1978 and ended as the school was earmarked for closure. More than 2,000 children and adults took part, with at least a quarter running for the Paycare charity. Ready to start are, from left to right, back row: Ruth Turner, Lauren Bryan, Gemma Spate, Jake Stringfellow-Powell, Rose Copson. Front row: Liz Price of Paycare, Stuart Sneade, Dave Bowyer, headmaster.

The Wrekin summit found itself the venue for a rally in December 2005 when three armoured vehicles and a 200-strong army of protesters assembled to express concern over their jobs and the future of military repair workshops at the Donnington Army depot in north Telford.

If hill walking is not possible, a helicopter ride is an unusual way of exploring The Wrekin. This view of the summit was taken from the south-west in June 2006. The Needle's Eye outcrop lies towards bottom left, while the south-western gate of the Iron Age hill fort is near the centre.

Right: George Evans, born in June 1923 and a staunch Wellingtonian, epitomises everyone who cherishes The Wrekin. He's considered by many to be the current 'Old Man of The Wrekin', although his visits to the summit aren't as frequent as they once were. Two books, *Secrets of the Wrekin Forest* and *Fern Ticket to the Magic Forest of the Wrekin* are part of his large collection of writings about Wellington's history and its surrounding countryside. George, a former town councillor, is life president of the Wellington Civic Society, and together with this author, provides historical information on the area to schools, colleges, newspapers, magazines, radio and television as well as anyone else who may be interested.

Below: The previous 'Old Man of The Wrekin' celebrates his ninetieth birthday in September 2005 with a champagne party at the summit. Allan Wedge of Wrockwardine climbed the hill every week from his teens until his death in 2008. From left to right: Graham Leddington, Dennis Morgan, Wynn Pryce, John Dooney, Allan Wedge (with his Jack Russell dog), Eric Biddulph.

Other local titles published by The History Press

Wellington in the 1940s and '50s
ALLAN FROST

This collection of archive photographs documents life in the historic Shropshire market town of Wellington during and after the Second World War. Entertaining and informative, this book reveals how the people of Wellington coped with severe rationing and how they found enjoyment in a wide range of activities. *Wellington in the 1940s and '50s* is an important pictorial history which will delight all who have lived or worked here.

0 7524 3767 4

Wellington in 1960
ALLAN FROST

Wellington was a thriving market town in 1960, serving the needs of neighbouring farming and industrial communities as well as its own inhabitants. This collection of archive photographs of the town is a unique snapshot of Wellington in the days when it held a position of historical and social importance in east Shropshire. *Wellington in 1960* is a nostalgic look at how the townspeople lived, worked and played at that time.

0 7524 2630 3

Around Shrewsbury Volume II
DEREK M. WALLEY

This collection of 200 archive pictures highlights some of the developments that have taken place in the county town of Shrewsbury during the last century. Important events are recalled, including a visit by King George V in 1914, alongside aspects of everyday life, from schools and churches to shops and local industry. Life in some of the surrounding villages is also remembered, including Acton Burnell, Dorrington, Longnor, Baschurch and Shawbury.

0 7524 3371 7

Shropshire Inn Signs
ALAN ROSE

Inn signs have been an enduring part of the British landscape for over 2,000 years and have provided the public with an illustrative depiction of the name of the pub outside which they hang. This book takes the reader on a tour of Shropshire's inns past and present, discovering the origins of names such as The Winning Post, The Trout and The Blue Boar. Illustrated with over 100 images, *Shropshire Inn Signs* offers a fascinating insight into the history of these highly crafted items.

0 7524 3843 3

If you are interested in purchasing other books published by The History Press, or in case you have difficulty finding any of our books in your local bookshop, you can also place orders directly through our website

www.thehistorypress.co.uk